# THE
# DREAM
# BOOK

## A Simple Guide to
## Interpreting Your Dreams

# STEVEN MADDOX

Published by Radiant Publishing
Paperback ISBN: 979-8-9865413-4-1
Ebook ISBN: 979-8-9865413-5-8

First Edition
Printed in the United States

Scan for a video from Steven!

# Dedication

I would like to dedicate this book to Ginny, my wife, for the countless hours of help and support along the way. I love and appreciate you more each day. I could not have written this book without you, and to my four children, Cassandra, Naomi, Luke, and Victoria, you make my world a better place.

# *Acknowledgments*

I want to thank John Paul Jackson for his friendship and countless hours of mentoring in understanding dreams and visions, and Harold Bredesen for his incredible wisdom and friendship and for helping me discover my purpose in life. Thank you, Jeremy and Ally Butrous, for helping me write this book. I would also like to thank my family, friends, and others who have supported me; you know who you are.

# FOREWORD

I stepped into the elevator of an event center restaurant with a new friend who wanted to do a quick segment with me for a social media show he was creating. He had brought another friend whom he was mentoring in his process of creating media, and as the three of us stood in the fast-moving elevator of one of the tallest buildings in Dallas, his friend looked at me and said, "I dreamed all of this before. You were in my dream." I love the lead-in of a good dream because I know how powerful dreams can be, so I smiled and said, "Tell me about it."

The dreamer was Steven Maddox, who is going to become an incredible mentor to you through this book, and he shared a dream about connecting with me in media. He had already created many entertainment projects but had transitioned to working on a show about spiritual dreams with one of the most renowned dream interpreters, John Paul Jackson. I had known John Paul pretty well, but I had never seen his show, although I had heard about it. Part of Steven's dream was about working with me on the late John Paul Jackson's show Dreams and Mysteries, which Steven was still producing and directing. When I got back to California, Steven texted me and asked if I wanted to help host Dreams and Mysteries.

Now, things get weird when you have someone like Steven contact you. Steven carries the atmosphere of faith for dreaming and understanding the purposes of your dreams. It's not just the thousands (if not 10K plus dreams) he has interpreted. He walks with God in a unique way, and I have learned to lean on him through the years with dreams and my process. But this was the beginning of the story. When I saw the text, my first reaction was, "No, I don't want to host a Christian faith-based TV show."

But then he sent me a picture of the set, and I was shocked. I have had a recurring dream of that set since I was a child over dozens of times. I was so impacted by this set that Steven and his wife, Ginny, had created I had to say yes. My dreams led me to a yes. And this led me into my current ministry and career change to produce and host content with Steven inspiring so many parts of it through the years.

Dreams are among the most recognized revelatory leaders in the lives of many influencers, business people, politicians, and pastors. As a matter of fact, one of the TV shows I have hosted for a few years now on CBN News (which also has a podcast) is called Exploring the Marketplace, where we talk to everyday career people about how their faith has made a difference in their world. In the production questionnaire we send our guests; we ask them if God has ever spoken to them in a way that moved their career forward. About one of every three guests shares a dream and how God used it to redefine something in their life or lead them in a direction they were not thinking about.

These conversations have shown me how important dreams are to humanity. Not only does the Bible share dreams from some amazing people and their interpretations, but it also gives us a unique vantage point that dreams are one of the primary ways God connects His thoughts, will, and love to us.

We hosted some dream classes with Steven and Ginny on our online Spiritual Growth Academy, which is a place for believers of all backgrounds to take on spiritual themes and gifts and see them implemented more strongly in their lives. The Maddox's classes were some of our most popular by far, and having so many people engage and interact with them, I knew two things:

1. Dreams are special, but not unique. They are one of the ways that God has made revelation available, especially to this generation right now.

2. Steven is an awesome teacher because he imparts from his spiritual authority the hunger to interpret and find meaning in your dream life. He feels like a father figure to dreamers because he knows it's not about his ability to interpret but ultimately yours.

This book that you hold in your hands is a key for you to unlock an incredible place of connection to God. The Dream Book is going to weave into the very fabric of your faith that your dreams are a powerful meeting place between you and Jesus. It will take you on a journey to learn that dreams are mostly about you and between you and God. It will help you to build your identity and also provide ways to look at symbols and metaphors in a more simplified manner.

If you have never interpreted dreams, or if they felt too complicated and you have pressed pause on finding meaning in your dream life, you have just moved forward by getting this book. As you read these pages, you are going to start finding yourself growing in spiritual hunger, discernment, and wisdom on what your dreams mean, and ultimately you are going to know yourself and God in a way that only a dreamer who dares to walk in the fullness of dreams does.

**Shawn Bolz**

Host of the Shawn Bolz show, Exploring the Marketplace, and Producer/Host at TBN of Discovering God and Translating God show. Author of Encounter, Translating God, God Secrets, and Breakthrough. Find Shawn on YouTube and Socials @shawnbolz.

# ENDORSEMENTS

A long-awaited book from the leading dream interpreter on the planet. In it, Steven Maddox has chosen to take us on an adventure ... using dreams to discover our true purpose in life. Amazing. Don't be surprised if you find your life changed forever.

**S. C. Mummert, Artist**


I love the way Steven describes the dreams that help us see ourselves. I've had hundreds, maybe thousands, of dreams over my 76 years. The most profound have been in the last 50 years when I became a Christian. Dreams have unlocked my deepest fears and reveal the doorway to my greatest freedom. Steven has many times helped me to simplify my dreams into usable instructions. I think this book will trigger and unlock some things about yourself that will free you to become the best version of yourself.

**Don Abshere, Mentor**


I am happy to endorse The Dream Book, written by my good friend Steven Maddox, for three essential reasons. First of all, Steven has been not just a strong practitioner of interpreting dreams for many years; he has actually been a pioneer in the modern ministry of dream interpretation. God has used Steven powerfully for decades in bringing insight, breakthrough, and healing to many, many people.

Secondly, Steven's treatise on dreams doesn't come across as so much a classroom lecture, but more like a great conversation with a friend and mentor. Steven writes as he lives – out of a high value of relationship! Lastly, Steven constantly reminds us that dreams never deals with us as simply part of a program. So the specific ways in which dreams will speak to each of us are in accord with the unique designs He has for each of us! The Dream Book will prove to be both an engaging read and a very helpful resource for life.

**Marc A. Dupont**
**Mantle of Praise Ministries, Inc.**


Steven Maddox dares to ask the compelling question, "Do you want a sense of purpose or a divine purpose?" Experiencing people who have become completely alive causes restlessness in us, wondering how they got there. In The Dream Book, Steven is a masterful guide connecting the deepest, untapped tool to communicate our pathway to purpose.... our dreams. Instead of waking up feeling exhausted by seemingly random symbols and scenarios, Steven demystifies the language that our minds are seeking to speak to us about our very own lives. In this absorbing book, he reveals a process to personally interpret your dreams in ways that will anchor you in your present, remove what's not life-giving, and direct you into the meaning of your divine purpose.

**Lauren Hasson**
**Founder and Director of Longitude 33**


Have you ever had one of those dreams where you travel to a remote place in the Himalayas, seeking a sage to inspire you toward your destiny? You probably don't want to look through one more dream dictionary to find the answer to your future, but you will find the guidance and wisdom you are looking for through the introspective reflections of The Dream Book by Steven Maddox. This thought-provoking roadmap to understanding dreams will illuminate a path for you to take the guesswork out of your night stories. If you have had one of those wise sages appear in your dream travels, look no further. Let Steven inspire you to find your destiny through your dreams.

**Rebecca Holihan**
**Executive Director of Springs Gate Ministries**

# CONTENTS

THE DREAM BOOK

# My Dream
# Encounter

I want to tell you about a dream I had, which is the reason that I wrote this book. In the dream, I was going somewhere I had never been before, but I intuitively knew the direction and began walking. I headed toward an overgrown wilderness with no path to follow.

It was a long journey through steep terrain and rocky patches of land that seemed full of endless searches, to no avail. I could see in the earth where the ancient boundaries had been crossed. I was determined to continue without violating the ancient boundaries, and found myself on an overgrown pathway hidden from those who didn't understand the ancient boundaries.

I knew this was part of my destiny to find the ancient doorway into a place that time seemed to have long been forgotten. I continued to forge ahead; however, I couldn't see more than a few feet in front of me most of the time. The path I was on seemed that no one had walked on for centuries. I heard a voice saying, "This is the way, walk in it." I followed the ancient boundaries for hours and hours. Then suddenly, I came to a summit and my vision was unobstructed. It seemed like I could see forever and, in high definition, extremely clear. I saw a structure in the distance and knew it was my destination. I was getting very close.

The land began to change the closer I got to the house. Surrounding this giant house is an iron fence with a locked gate. The iron fence and gate are 12 feet high and impossible to climb. There is a way to enter, but you must have a key. The keyhole looks like an ancient key would be the type of key needed. Where would I be able to find this key out here in a meadow of rolling hills? As I was looking through the gate, I could see the house. The walls were made of stone and seemed as if it was here before time began. It looked like an actual fortress with turrets and walls as high as I could see.

There was light shining brightly throughout the house and windows all around. I reached into my pocket to grab my keys to see if any would fit the lock, and as I touched my keys they changed shape, and I could unlock the gate. The courtyard was a place of reflection with pools of water and places to rest. It seemed like it took me a lifetime to enter this world, so I rested and looked at the house/fortress in awe and wonder.

I got up and walked over to touch the wall. The stones were massive and cut perfectly to fit together. I began to walk around the fortress looking for a way to enter, but I couldn't find one. I knew the overgrowth of vines, trees, and plants were blocking the doorway that had to be there. It took me a while to find the hidden door covered in overgrowth. I was cutting back the vines and trees for hours. Once I could see the door, I had to dig the bottom of it out. It was buried in at least a foot of earth. After it was cleared, I still had difficulty opening the door and had to use a pry bar.

The door measured 14 feet high and 7 feet wide, an ancient door that had not been opened in thousands of years. Once I opened the door and went through it, I felt a personal mission to take others through it. The door had been closed for so long that I had to fix it to close and open it again. I had to cut the bottom of the door at a right angle so that it would open because the earth around it had changed its shape.

As I entered the house, I was in the entryway looking at a timepiece when I was handed an open book. It was an ancient book and it seemed that it was written before time began. Although the book was open, most of it was "sealed" and unreadable at first as I scrolled through the pages. The book was written in a translucent font you could see through, and you would need special training to see all the colors to read it. I read through the book a few times before my eyes opened and could finally read the language it was written in. I could feel God's presence on, around, and in the book. As my eyes adjusted, I also saw that the pages were translucent. The words/letters came off the pages and became alive. I was breathing in the language, and it was becoming part of my being. As my eyes opened more, I could read the stories.

While reading, the pages were giving off orbs of light and Spirit. The deeper I got into it, the more I witnessed light, life, and history particles coming off the pages. This effect was continuous, but the book never changed. It seemed to be an endless book of unveiling. I could smell the language as I read it. I was breathing in its life, light, and essence all at the same time. It seemed like my understanding was being opened to comprehend the revelation of this book. The book was dream language, the oldest language known to us, and I was taught how to read and understand it. I will open the door for you...

# THE DREAM BOOK

# INTRODUCTION
# TO DREAMS

Welcome to the mystical, fantastic, symbolic, and extraordinarily practical dream world! Here you will find answers to the secrets of your heart and uncover your purpose! A word of caution! This book is a very different dream book from those you have probably seen or read.

In a dream, I found myself running in an open maze faster than I could in real life. There were many around me running just as fast. Then, we all made a crazy jump over the chasm onto a rope ladder that went miles into the clouds. Right and left, as quickly as my arms could climb, I lifted myself higher and higher. In a matter of seconds, I arrived at the front porch of my own house! I opened the door and saw the living room, kitchen, bathroom, and hallway. They were not just rooms with people and things; each room had a message for me. Each piece of furniture told me something about myself. In the living room, I stood and looked at the couch. I knew the loveseat could only seat three people naturally, but there were 18 people on it. I knew inside my heart that I carried 18 people as close friends and family, and I saw all 18 of them on the couch. Then I looked up at the TV and saw re-runs and commercials that matched the messages I tell myself all the time and what I believe about myself.

The carpet, temperature, lighting, pictures, furniture, and every noticeable element of the room were talking to me simultaneously and telling me things about myself. I went into a living house that knew me and wanted to share facts about me. The personal, deep, intimate parts of my life were superimposed over each room. The messages were all around. I learned things about myself in each room as the dream continued, which seemed to last for eight or more hours, in each room. I had this dream in stages for three consecutive nights. Allow me to introduce you to the Dream House. I will be your guide and show you around throughout the remainder of this book.

Now, let's get down to the brass tacks! Your pocket prophet is no longer needed to help you dream and interpret your dreams. You will be able to interpret your dreams after reading this book. After having and personally interpreting thousands of dreams, I have learned a few things that I would love to share with you. We are going to look at the core elements of a dream. Where do dreams come from? What are the actual benefits of dreams? How can we have more dreams and apply them to our lives?

When dreaming and interpreting, we will look at people's current pitfalls, struggles, and roadblocks. In my generation, dream dictionaries were a thing, and people would search for a word or meaning and have no idea how to apply it to their lives. People spend lots of time guessing, googling, and forgetting. For most, the actual benefits of dreams are a fun conversation at breakfast. Dreams are so much more!

I want to teach you how to become the best dreamer and self-interpreter. This book will give you a more perfected roadmap on how to interpret your dreams! Dreams can save you time and money. They can keep you out of bad relationships and help you find a job, a house, and even your spouse. Dreams can access the core processor of our thoughts, affections, emotions, and will;

because of this, they are and can be integral to the fabric of what makes us who we are. When you wake from a profound dream and check in with yourself, you may notice your heart has changed a small percentage about something. When our heart changes, our actions change. When you have a thought-provoking dream, you may be left thinking and processing about a person, place, or situation differently. Dreams spark our everyday realities. Dreams can be and should be a catalyst in our lives.

Dreams are profound, fun, brutally honest, mysterious, lovely, revealing, life-changing, helpful, meaningful, and most of all, dreams are us. They can embody every emotion and speak to the very core of who we are. They are, by design, a plumb line to help us discover ourselves and the world around us.

Dreams can affect every area of our lives; here are a few common areas of life we may dream about:

- **Relationships**
  - People often have dreams about habits that they need to change in their relationships.

- **Subtle things**
  - Your life is filled with subtle things that need your attention, and dreams reveal our life's subtleties.

- **Life-changing things**
  - For starters, dreams are filled with life-changing directions like whom to marry, where to live, and where to work.

- **Transitions**
  - Everyone has transitions in their lives, going from one season to the next. We all grow up and need direction. We need to see into the next season, and dreams help us get there.

- **Financial things**
  - ◦ Finances are inherently connected to who we are, and we dream about them often. Dreams about our finances can help us make better decisions and keep us from some bad ones.

- **Save your time**
  - ◦ Dreams can help us process and cut through the noise, save time, and be more efficient.

- **Keep you out of trouble**
  - ◦ Warnings are a crucial way we listen to our dreams. Dreams can keep us from going down the wrong path in life.

- **Situation specific**
  - ◦ Dreams can be particular to help us improve specific situations.

Dreams can be complex, and learning a new dream language can be challenging. Therefore dreams need a roadmap to understand, not a dictionary. Dreamers need a guide to show them how to learn how to dream and interpret on their own. I will be your guide. I will use my history, perspective, and tools to teach you what I know about how to be a better dreamer and interpreter. I am unapologetically a Christian and will use old testament and new testament examples to expound on the nature and origins of dreams, but this book is for everyone. If you are a dreamer or want to be one, there are many things you can learn in this book.

We will discover together that dreams are one of the best built-in communication tools with yourself. The primary purpose of dreams is to guide, direct, and caution you into the purpose and meaning of your life. Also, our unconscious and preconscious mind wants to talk to us all the time through dreams. They share random facts with us, not necessarily about realities or certainties all the time, but also about our fears, emotions, and thoughts. We can get to know ourselves in profound and meaningful ways through dreams.

Dreams can tell us if we overlook an essential detail in a business decision. How about a sneak peek at the deep-seated fears and doubts affecting your relationships? What about a problem at work that you have had trouble solving?

Dreams provide insight and gentle nudges to help us learn about ourselves and the people around us. Dreams aren't just for special people. They are for everyone. This dream world will transcend your everyday language and teach you a new way to understand your nightlife. You will discover who you are and have a lot of amazing dreams along the way. If you have never had a dream before, this book is for you. Suppose you have been dreaming all of your life and read 100 dream books; then this book is for you too.

A few things you will learn in this book:

- The goal of your dreams.
- How to self-interpret your dreams in repeatable ways.
- How to discover your purpose in more profound and meaningful ways.
- The fundamental skills to teach yourself and others to self-interpret.
- A new language to unlock your dreams.

Over the years, I have noticed that people tend to look at dreams in either a passive, non-applicable way or in a literal sense. Read this quick example about Suzy and Jenny, and think about which one you are. Suzy dreamt about a snake sliding into her purse when she arrived home. She tells herself that dream was stupid, forgets about it, and goes on with her life. Jenny dreamt about a snake crawling into her purse, and she called the exterminator, googled local snakes in the area, and checked how much anti-venom is in the local hospitals based on the snakes she imagined. Two very different approaches to the dream! We will learn who is correct in their interpretation later in the book. We will also discuss the proper way to look at your dreams so you know what should be taken literally and what should be interpreted as symbolic. We will also evaluate what elements of your dreams you should learn from and which ones you should throw away.

It's incredible to me that our culture, for the most part, does not embrace dreams. In the past, we have had some of the brightest minds who understood that dreams could change everything, create everything, and help us understand everything. It's time for dreams to be taught in a meaningful way that brings real practical change and application.

There has been a cultural understanding that dreams are invisible, spiritual, and non-practical, which continues to separate dreamers from the potential they could achieve in life if they understood the true purpose of dreams. If they only knew dreams are an extension of us, not some foreign entity in the cosmos or some untethered rogue imagination. We will discover in this book that dreams are as real as our personalized DNA. You were born to be a dreamer. It is a gift that can be cultivated, nurtured, and grown. Welcome to the fantastic world of dreams!

## House warming gift

Dreams have a natural relationship with our lives. What better way to teach dreams than to look at the dream house in which we discover rooms that lead us to the discovery of ourselves? The correlation between our natural and dreamer selves is profound, and we will see this layout in each dream house room. I will frequently show you rooms inside my dream house and break it down for you to see what's inside. The fundamentals of what we are about to do will be discussed in the following chapters. If this seems silly to you, follow along; for now, I assure you it will be worth it! Follow along with me into the kitchen.

I slowly walk into my kitchen and notice everything. I could see the Spanish ceramic tiles on the floor, feel the 74-degree temperature in the room, and see which lights were turned on. I only like the light on over the stove because it is calming, but it has enough light to get things done. This is where I meet with my family and have fellowship with my friends. I prepare small snacks over there by the window cupboards. Sometimes we have mixed nuts and dry cereal out to snack on. I also make coffee with my wife on the stove over there. We like it strong; French press roast brought to 195 degrees with medium roast beans from Guatemala. It's an intimate space for me. Sometimes I talk about the most profound things in my heart in my kitchen.

I often communicate more with others in my kitchen than in other rooms. Ginny, my wife, and I always offer something to our guests in our kitchen. It's a habit; we like to be hospitable. I remember the last meal I cooked here with my wife. I stood by, and she did most of the work, but I helped. It was a salad filled with many healthy things: arugula, pecans, corn, tomatoes, cheese, and pomegranate seeds. I do love making things with my wife!

Take a look over here on the corner of the wall. It is a marker that we use to measure the growth of each of our kids. We would put their backs up against the wall each year and mark the top of their head to see how much they had grown. Seeing these memories and how much they have grown up is fun.

## What is your kitchen saying?

Now, did you notice what my dream kitchen means to me? I could see fellowship, intimacy, communication, sharing, friendship, growth, memories, nutrition, and much more. The colors of the tile, the space in the fridge, the brightness of the lights, and the tone of the conversations all mean something. They are all speaking to me and sharing information with me. It's like the room itself is alive and is talking to me in a creative artistic way, a symbolic way.

I have an idea of what harmony is in my kitchen. In my dreams, I know when things are all in their correct place. If something is off, I am aware enough to spot it, and the displacement should tell me something. If I see a broken tile on the floor, it tells me something. I am learning something if the coffee only comes out cold, no matter how long I leave it on the stove. Perhaps the lights flicker for seven minutes when I turn them on. What message is that sending me? In dreams, everything is essential until it's not. Sometimes the tiny details that are missed or overlooked hold the keys to understanding and application.

Dreams are not always in plain speech. I just told you about my kitchen. It's a composite of my real kitchen and the kitchen I see in my dreams. Sure there could be quotes or messages written on the walls or even spoken during a dream, but my environment is the message more often than not. The people in the room are the message. Sometimes, the people missing from the room are the message. Messages are veiled in sight for the keen and interested, like little clues to a lifelong puzzle. We will return to the dream house in a bit after we discuss your participation and worth.

# Big picture

Just like our natural life, dreams require user participation. Why? Because you are made different, and you have a purpose beyond what you can comprehend. It's essential to find out a little about yourself before we can see the value in dreams because if we think we are the scum of the earth up to no good, then how valuable will our dreams be? They will be worthless, maybe pointless.

You were born different from everyone else, aside from the idea of people creating people, which is crazy awesome. The odds of you being here reading this book are perhaps incalculable. Let's consider the odds between your parents; it is a mind-blowing number. On average, your mother has about 300,000 eggs to fertilize after puberty, and your father produces roughly 525 billion sperm cells in his lifetime. Let's say 250 million sperm are sent out at once, which would be about 75 trillion odds, and the probability of only 20% of the eggs being fertilized brings our number to about 400 trillion. You are one in 400 trillion! It is much more than that because your parents would have had the same odds as your grandparents, great-grandparents, and great-great-grandparents. You get the idea. You should feel exceptional to have made it this far! The odds of you being here and reading this book on dreams are incalculable!

So you are a miracle, different from every other world miracle. Your DNA is one of a kind set to you, and no one else shares it. Your eyes, fingerprints, toes, ears, lips, and tongue are all unique to you only. No one else is the same! You were made different, and that was the plan! You have something special inside of you. You have defeated the odds of being born. You are fearfully and wonderfully made!

When building a dream world worth exploring, one must start by looking at the dreamer. Just like you, no two dreams are the same. Dreams are made for you. No two dreams are alike because they are made for the dreamer. Without the dreamer, no dreams would exist. Okay, simple concept, but it is incredibly profound when applied. Why are you so special to have this dream? Why are you having the dream over your neighbor or someone 50 years from now in a different country? The answer is you. You are something special to be alive and receive dreams.

## Why am I so special?

Great question! Why are you even here? What is the point of all of this? Look at how unique our species is, our ability to create, build, grow, and adapt. We are exceptional for millions and millions of reasons. Why did I defeat all of the odds? Who am I? Why are we even here? What is my place or unique contribution to this world? What is my purpose? Open your mind and consider that you were born into a world you did not know. You had zero; I mean zero control over your ability to be born. Your understanding did not make that happen as impressive as it is. Something much more significant than your understanding of the facts brought you here.

We are born for a purpose that transcends our ability to comprehend at times. It is for purpose's sake that we dream. Our dreams' communication has meaning, and in that meaning, we find life! It feeds, teaches, and guides us in how we should go. Most dreams are small puzzle pieces in the puzzle of our life. They usually point to who we are and what we are about.

Knowing your purpose is foundational to understanding your dreams, and understanding your dreams is foundational to knowing your purpose. This is a catch-22 type of situation. We're in a dilemma from which there seems to be no escape. A mutual conflict and reward are tied between your dreams and your purpose. However, as you go through this book, it will get you through this.

I believe our dreams are 80-90% connected to our purpose, calling, and destiny, even the throwaway dreams. We will go over our different dreams and why later in the book. Nevertheless, I believe we have dreams to keep us on track in this life. When you buy a new car, they ask if you want navigation built in for an extra cost. We are given navigation at birth, and dreams are a big way to guide us to our destination, purpose, and calling.

Knowing your purpose may not seem related to the subject of dreams, but this is the foundation of understanding your dreams. This took me a long time to figure out. But, after interpreting dreams for years, I started to see patterns connected to the person and what they were doing. The dreamer seems to be unequivocally connected to the dreams. Tons of dreams pointed to a nuanced understanding of why they were here and their calling.

The more I considered this connection, the more the dream world opened up for me to see and understand. Seeing the purpose of a dream helps me put together the fundamental pieces of how dreams work. There is one primary question I discovered in all of my explorations. How do I interpret and understand my dreams if I don't know my purpose? It is a challenging proposition and can be very confusing, which is where most dreamers are at.

We will look at ways to find out why you are here and what you were designed to do to assist us in interpreting your dreams. Your dreams are connected to your destiny! So to know what your dreams tell you, you must first know who you are and what you're here for. We can't make it through this life without knowing who we are, and thank God we don't have to.

The epiphany of knowing what you were born to do is the greatest thing that will ever happen to you! Knowing settles many issues in our lives and brings wholeness to our entire being. Knowing what you were born to do aligns with your walk and decisions. Think about this for a moment; we are purely a miracle created in this time zone in humanity with a specific purpose! There is something for us to become, participate with, and do in this life that brings us fulfillment. Perhaps a north star is guiding us all in the multitude of billions of choices. Perhaps, everyone is connected in some way or another to a higher purpose inspired daily by the divine. I believe so, and my life is a testament to that.

Understanding your life's purpose could take some time, but I bet your dreams will help you find some of the answers you have been looking for. Dreams are a communication tool to tell us about ourselves. They help us build upon the foundation of our identity. They guide and reinforce the way you should go. Dreams are essential in your personal development. Our understanding of this process only accelerates our growth but is not essential in this happening regardless.

The primary purpose of our dreams is to keep us walking toward our purpose. Dreams will remind you of your gifts, talents, and abilities first and foremost. Then, if you're not using your gifts, talents, and abilities, dreams will also direct, instruct and warn you. Our purpose is the basis of all our dreams. The plumb line of purpose is so critical to any self-defining process because it is what anchors us into something. Without it, we change like the wind and have no footprint or application in life.

Our purpose is not fluffy speech; it's what provides us with meaning. A friend of mine, Dr. Ally Butrous, helped me compose a few key identifiers in what defines our purpose, divine purpose, true purpose, and our sense of purpose. She is a doctor in psychology with way too much education. Thank you, Dr. Ally!

## Divine/true purpose vs. a sense of purpose

Our purpose is composed of two key areas. Our true/divine purpose and our sense of purpose. Divine purpose is foundational; it's long-lasting, trustworthy, and a source of life. Our sense of purpose can be fickle, passive, and changing. It's good to recognize the type of purpose you draw from (strength, perspective, and energy) to know where you're going.

The following list includes common denominators to help us understand our purpose. These traits overlap with our divine purpose and our sense of purpose in different ways. It is up to us to distinguish and separate them appropriately. The division of ourselves is not an all-or-nothing approach; there will always be overlap, and this is not an exhaustive list.

- Natural/physical gifting
- Spiritual gifting
- Talents and abilities
- Developed skill sets
- Desires
- Passions
- Callings
- What you love to do
- Born into or born for
- Education
- What are you internally driven to do
- What bothers you the most

These purpose denominators give us clues about who we are today. They help us understand our hearts, actions, and intentions. Now, let's take an assessment of these and pair them with our divine purpose. We will notice holes or vacancies in our understanding or application. That's okay; it's good to have an honest assessment of where you are today. Our true purpose is built around the divine. Why? Because *our understanding can't be the standard that defines our humanity. We don't even agree with our neighbors on most things. Our history as humans is filled with wars and disagreements because so much of the "right" thing to do varies based on limited individual perspectives. Social nets produce different laws and social norms to abide by that differ from state to state and country to country. We can't control what happens when we fall asleep and dream, and we sure have no idea where Tupac is. We have to accept that not only do we not know it all, but we might not even be fully conscious of why we do anything or think how we think.*

*Here is a list of identifiers to help us see our divine purpose.*

*Divine/True Purpose:*
1. *Our Divine Purpose comes from Godly values, promises, mandates, and prophecy, all geared to bring us life.*
2. *Our Divine Purpose brings noticeably good fruit to the people around us in small and big ways.*
3. *Our Divine Purpose is recognizable to the people around us as something that is part of our life/calling.*
4. *Our Divine Purpose grows because of how we do something, even more than what we do.*
5. *Our Divine Purpose is mirrored by the life and eternal purpose of Jesus.*
6. *Our Divine Purpose brings meaning and a compounding "good" to our life.*
7. *Our Divine Purpose is built on established truth, not feelings.*
8. *Our Divine Purpose is rarely short-term in application because God is eternal.*
9. *Our Divine Purpose is something you invest your time, talents, and gifts into, not something that comes out of nowhere.*
10. *Our Divine Purpose should create compounding feelings of satisfaction and enjoyment as we invest in it.*

*Our Divine purpose guides our purpose. Within this framework, we have the most control and choice. That is why we are guided, not forced. Dreams become the constant voice that speaks to us regardless of our listening. Our participation is not diminished by this but expanded. We also find purpose in other ways, some good and some not-so-good. That is what I call the sense of purpose. We must be mindful of our Sense of Purpose and keep it in check with our True and Divine purpose. We can find good in our Sense of Purpose, but it can also lead us astray.*

*Here is a non-exhaustive list of some ways we find our sense of purpose.*

*Sense of Purpose:*
1. *Through camaraderie, our connection to people.*
2. *Through feelings of security.*
3. *Through following rules because of predictable outcomes.*
4. *Through Association and who we align with.*
5. *Through feeling good at the moment, without considering consequences or long term.*
6. *Through the feeling of being important to others, fear of losing them.*
7. *Through the feeling of pleasure. It comes and goes depending on the day.*
8. *Through feelings of happiness. It comes and goes depending on the day.*
9. *It can be something you hope will happen to you.*
10. *You spend more time thinking about how others will like/admire/ perceive you for what you are doing.*

*Hopefully, you can see the distinctions between your true/divine purpose and our sense of purpose. They don't need to be mutually exclusive; our sense of purpose can be from a good place. We need to keep the bit in our mouth so we are guided by our true purpose and not get taken off course with feelings that can be more temporal and fickle.*

*Our dreams are geared to reaffirm our purpose and calling in life. They will speak to and direct us to keep us in our purpose throughout life, just like a guardrail on the highway. We are to stay the course. If we go in the wrong direction, our dreams will tell us if we are listening. Purpose-centric understanding is essential to our dream lives. If we detach our purpose from the interpretation of our dreams, then we are left to reading dictionaries and guess. We would, in essence, be detaching from ourselves. Who is more qualified to know about you than you are? No one, not your doctor, mom, pastor, or your friend!*

*You may not know your purpose or what you were called to do yet. Let me tell you some good news. That is also why you dream! You dream of discovering these things about yourself! It's time to confirm the correlations of others about your talents and abilities. It's time to see yourself through your true purpose and start living it out in more meaningful ways. Dreams will help you see who you were born to be. Let's start dreaming.*

# SPAGHETTI
# ON THE WALL

The Google era has brought us some fantastic things; however, searching for dream interpretation online is more counter-productive than any good. Imagine grabbing a massive plate of spaghetti, then throwing it on the wall to see what picture comes out. That is the same as having a dream and then typing it on Google.

What objectives would one seek to find in searching for their dream answers? Comparison, commonality, popular opinion, and expert insight. Which one of these is established on the fundamentals of understanding you? None, perhaps. Just because someone wrote a book on dream definitions doesn't make it applicable to you and your dream. The same would go for popular opinion pieces. They are attractive, emotional, and sometimes fun to read, but how could our baseline dream interpretation come from people with whom we have very little connection?

That's right, your dictionary books, symbol books, and quick reference guides are only as good as your own personal agreement. Personal agreement is when you bring a thought into ownership within yourself and find identifying traits therein. Imagine having a dream about a lion. If you were born before 1991, you reach under your bed, next to your extra phone charger, and grab your handy dandy dream interpretation symbols book. You flip right over to the "L" section to find out what lions mean. Hmm, cunning, kings of their domain, cat family. You say to yourself, "Wow! Let's start stringing this thing together. We have some facts to line up with. I am called to be a king, and I love cats; I do like some cunning lions in movies. Okay. Dream interpreted." Wrong! How could a dictionary or quick reference guide speak to your individuality, needs, will, thoughts, and current life and give you an accurate interpretation? It's like throwing spaghetti on the wall.

"Standardize me" is the hope of many teachers and manufacturers. How can one process be taught and applied to everyone so we can maximize impact and returns? In the case of dreams, an individual interpretation process is out the window because the gifted man or woman is not there to interpret your dream. The solution was to standardize the external process to set the guide rails for all presiding interpretations through the development of dream dictionaries and books on dream symbols. The external is anything not coming from your own process but a principle you are told to adhere to.

The teacher would say, "Let's standardize the lion, so everyone knows what a lion is when they see one. Anytime you see a lion in your dream, look at this set of definitions to guide your interpretation." Spaghetti on the wall! We may get it right every once in a while and call it a win if we interpret one out of every 30 dreams with this approach. But what about the 29 that were a miss? Not a very good completion percentage. Why is this not a promising approach for the end user? Standardization does not work in dream interpretation unless a personal agreement has been achieved. Again, a personal agreement is when you bring a thought into ownership within yourself and find identifying traits therein. We will cover more on this later.

You have now been set free from your symbols dictionary! You're welcome! If you are still looking to donate, there are lots of excellent charitable organizations available. When searching for new books in the future and seeing a shiny new dream dictionary, slap yourself and say, "No dictionary knows me better than I do." Then run away, like Tom Hanks in Forrest Gump. The person authoring this shiny new dream dictionary may be well-intentioned, but they work from an archaic model that will leave you stuck and confused.

Principles should never take you away from the person. What I mean is that you should never let a rule keep you from a personal understanding of your dreams. Also, we should not be ignorant to the fact that we have guiding principles, symbols, and dreams that teach us. We are not starting in the clouds of our untethered ideas when we interpret. Definition-based dream books can provide us with a starting point to learn and grow. We can learn from guiding principles and not be held back by them.

## Hallway

As we continue through the Dream House, I would like to take you into another room. Let's go from the living room into the hallway. As I enter the hallway, it's relatively dark until I can find the light switch. Sometimes it's hard to find the switch, so I walk through without the light on. I know other rooms are connected to the hallway, but sometimes they are not in plain sight until I walk further. I know there are several rooms, an office, bathrooms, attic access, and a closet. In the  hallway are pictures of people that I have loved through the years. I also have pictures of things I want to remember that are beautiful or inspiring to me. Family pictures from past trips. My wedding. My extended family and kids. I can see pictures of my past or cherished moments with my family and friends. Times in my life that I hold near and dear to my heart, like my achievements. I like to see the high watermarks in my life and the memories of others on my walls. They are all about eye level, so I can reflect on them as I walk by.

In my hallway, there is nowhere to sit. It's a transitional space. It's only for going from one place to the other. If I find myself here, it's because I am going through it. When I am in my hallway, I think of time and how valuable it is—also the seasons of life and the seasons of people in my life. I also think of who I was and who I desire to be because of my memories posted on the wall. Lastly, and perhaps the most important consideration of the hallway, is transition. Transition is going from one place to another, going from one season to another, or even going from one job to another.

I am learning how I see myself based on my dream and real life. It's true, I do put up family pictures on the wall, and my intentions in my hallway are to pass through but sometimes be reminded of things like who I was or where I am going. Sometimes when I go back to my hallway in dreams, I feel like I can't see the other side. It's dark. I know I am to pass through. If I look at my memories, oftentimes, I am reminded that I am a new person or a better person now than who I was then. I face loss and regret, but I also cherish the wonderful and what I am proud of. I am learning how a hallway could be profound and enlightening if I see my life through the dream house!

## How is this different?

A few decades ago, I found myself traveling and interpreting dreams worldwide. One day I said, "I can't do this anymore. I can't die for this." I was teaching about dreams and was focused on interpreting the dreams of others, which seemed harmless until I started to understand that most people don't know their dream language. It can be pointless or even dangerous for them if I or anyone else interprets their dream. The primary approach was the complete reliance on a stranger to provide interpretation with a practical application. It weighed heavy on my heart. So much so that I walked away from it all. I realized it was probably the most significant waste of time in my life once I learned how our process of understanding dreams unlocks our ability to interpret them.

Sometime later, I began to study again, teach a little, and look at my notes when I had an epiphany! I had been doing it wrong the whole time. I was a part of a culture of people walking around with dream journals, talking about their dreams, and trying to figure them out, which turned out to be a big waste of time. If the dreamer was lucky, they would talk to someone gifted enough to sort the facts for them and give them a proper interpretation. However, that did not happen all the time. Dreamers would ask their friends for interpretation, and their friends would feel a sense of purpose in trying to help the dreamer and tell them what they thought they needed to hear.

The broken cycle of interpretation was centered around people spending hours going over and over the same things. The goals of the dreams were lost in the details. The dreamer did not define their types of dreams and each dream would be bundled in with the last. Any foundation they built would hide behind a simplistic good or bad approach, real or fake conclusion. I want to save you the trouble of making the same mistakes and make it simple.

Dreamers need a guide to teach them a few things about themselves, properly define the goals within dreams, and help define their own dream language. If any of these core ingredients are missing, then it's like a baby hearing words for the first time. Personal meaning, understanding, and response will be pretty limited. In the next chapter, we will discuss in great length our dream language. Without it, you will be back to guessing or calling up your friends about what they think black curtains mean.

We will also look at where dreams come from and why. What are dreams made of? What can dreams do? And how to approach dreams. We will go up into the clouds with some concepts and down into the very nitty-gritty details on others because I am your guide, and I don't want you to be lost.

## Unconsciousness, Preconscious, and Conscious State

Everyone has the ability to use their imagination (the central government of images in the nation of your mind) and pull from different forms of time, as well. Think of one of your favorite meals when you were a kid. Ahh, do you remember the pancakes, donuts, and cereal? Now, what was the last thing you ate? Was it breakfast? Can you feel it? Smell it? Can you see the dish in detail? If you and a friend go for a meal next week at your favorite restaurant, will you order your favorite dish? The one you have had many times before? Can you see it? Can you see both of you sitting down and enjoying this meal? Fantastic! You just used your imagination, mixed with memory and consciousness, simultaneously. You were operating in the unconscious, preconscious, and conscious state all at once.

Every day we pull our realities from a reservoir of the unconscious, conscious, and perhaps preconscious realms. We may pull our realities from all three realms all at the same time! Can someone control their unconscious and preconscious mind so much as to keep it at bay, while only entertaining their conscious? The conscious is not always the ultimate decision maker, but more of a "last stop on the bus u-turn bus route" heading back to the terminal of unconsciousness with a quick stop at the preconscious on the way.

The imagination can also create. Imagine a red balloon. Now, a giant red balloon. You saw it didn't you? Some felt it, some saw the wind blowing it back and forth. Some saw an inflated balloon, some a popped balloon. Some of you went back in history to see if you could recall one, and some created a new one with the elements of their personal truth about red balloons. Your imagination made that red balloon possible!

This is the reality we all live in on a daily basis, and it is also how we dream. Dreams are inserted in between the layers of consciousness, and sometimes, they are layered upon all three layers at the same time. That is why you can daydream right now! It is also why you dream at night and do not remember anything but know you did. And you also dream fantastic dreams at night with various elements like the present day, real people, and otherworldly universes.

When your imagination is fully active it's working continuously. It helps you bridge the gap between your layers of consciousness to help you fill in the gaps, practically and creatively. It's when you pull down your known truths about what you remember about a situation or person. Sometimes the details are a bit of a mess, so your imagination helps complete the thought process. The same thing happens in dreams, except the origins of your dreams could be pulled from life-changing places. Perhaps from divine places, God, self-will, and our future, to name a few.

## The build-up of the mail room in our minds

The mind is projected to consciously think about 30,000-70,000 thoughts each day. That is a lot of thoughts and is slightly under one thought per second. Let's think of our thoughts as mail.

That's a lot of "mail" to sort in the mailroom of our mind. In order to break the noise, we fill our minds each day with fears, lists, hesitations, reservations, conversations, emotions, plans, hopes, aspirations, self projections, etc., and abundant noise. Thoughts also compound and repeat based on our inability to bring each one to a resolution that satisfies our layers of consciousness. Each day's unanswered thoughts, feelings, etc., builds into the next day or gets lost. Our collective "mailroom" can become a big unwieldy mess!

Sometimes mail is sent up from the mailroom, and sometimes we send it down. However, the more unsorted mail we have, the more difficult it is to sort through our dreams and conscious thoughts. Sometimes there's so much mail in the mailroom of our unconscious mind it spills over into our dream lives. This would be a nightmare! Some might also call these "Pizza" dreams. You may ask yourself, "What in the world did I just dream? Mumbo jumbo mess dream, or a 'Pizza' dream." Perhaps you have heard about garbage pizza made popular in the midwest of the USA? It's pizza where they throw on every single topping available and call it garbage pizza.

How does one find direction, guidance, purpose, plans, and wisdom in all of the chaos? Indeed something has to bypass the crazy that we have and help us through it. I am delighted to tell you that we are not stuck without hope. Built within our fascinating design, we have a built-in secret door with easy access to every part of who we are. This is a bypass door that leads straight to the mailroom deep within our conscious and subconscious that communicates to us deeply, profoundly, and resolutely to help guide us in the way we should go. It's where dreams come from.

Sometimes we need to be "knocked out" fast asleep for this door to open because we have so much going on in our hearts and minds. Think of all of those examples in your personal life when you went to bed and woke up feeling like a "new person"? The bypass door was opened; perhaps you received some instruction, comfort, and peace. Did you know Adam in Genesis, the first book in the Bible, had to be "knocked out" fast asleep before God's dream of Eve could come about through Adam? We all experience this. Dreams help us listen when we are asleep because we would not or could not during the day. This is precisely why we need dreams. Dreams bypass any noise that may impede our ultimate purpose.

## Series of Cords

Allow me to take you on a little rabbit trail. I thought to myself, where do dreams come from? I ask myself, do dreams come from our bodies? Yes. Do they come from our Spirit? Yes. Do they come from our soul? Yes. Can you set up dreams outside of these three realms? Let's look at some Spirit, soul, and body dream examples.

Body dreams: these are dreams that come from your body. If you're sick, you can dream about how you feel physically. Our physical body can really affect our dreams. If you have the flu, this can really impact the type of dreams you'll have, as well as, if you take medication for the sickness. Let's say you have a broken arm; because of the pain in your arm, you could have a dream about your arm. These types of dreams are just processing what the body is going through. It's also interesting to note that if you're pregnant, this can impact your dreams because the baby, once it's developed enough, is dreaming, and while you are dreaming, things can get mixed up.

Soul dreams: these are dreams that come from your wants and desires. These dreams will be filled with the things that you want out of life, e.g. a car, house, or money. In these types of dreams you would get the car you want, the house you want, etc. You may have a dream and be asked to play guitar in a band because you're the best guitarist in the world. These types of dreams are pretty easy to notice, and they're really connected to your wants and desires. These are not the types of dreams that we're going to be talking about in this book.

Spirit dreams: these are dreams that come from God. It's easy to notice these dreams because they usually call us to something greater than we are or ever thought we could be. Joseph, from the Bible, dreamed he was going to be the leader of his family, and he was the youngest son. This seems like a soul dream because how could that be? It doesn't make any sense. But this is what he was called to do and who he was called to be. It was more significant than anything he could have imagined. Healthy God dreams will always call you up to a higher place in your life and into your calling. Part of spiritual dreams is that they bring correction to how we perceive ourselves and others. God has a plan for our life. These dreams will guide us to that plan and even show us the plan.

Spirit, soul, and body are all very connected. So much so that any division of them can only be done by God, and even He divides them together, not apart. The division is straight through all three, not in-between. Perhaps that's irrelevant to some, but we cannot begin to separate bodies from our emotions, can we? They are connected, one and the same. We cannot separate our souls from our minds or our spirits from our hearts. They are connected for a reason.

What is the reason? So we can hear from all three, and because they speak to each other. Did you know your internal organs don't have feelings? Often, when something is going on in your internal organs, you may see signs in different places in your body.

The same thing happens with our dreams; our physical health affects our dream life. Our spiritual life can affect our physical health, etc. This is a small way in which the interconnectedness of our lives helps us to dream and why we dream. The health of our mind, will, and emotions can affect how we dream, how often we dream, and what we dream about.

I know we can receive dreams directly from God, the devil, pizza, and a handful of other ways. Do they just come from wherever? What is the common denominator? I know we are not just recipients of our dreams; sometimes, we play a role in our dreams. I realized our dreams don't just happen without our participation or initiation, although sometimes they do. Our dreams are uniquely tied to us.

After researching and sorting through a large number of past dreams, it all started to make so much sense. I looked at the corresponding elements that are tied to our spirit, soul, and body because we are so intimately connected to those. We are a set of three cords that are not easily broken. Then, I realized the deep connection to where dreams come from is in a set of cords. Our soul can connect itself to things like hope and promise. We can also be personally tied to the soul of another through actions and agreements. We can be set free from the cords of people who wish to harm us. We can be bound by the cords of our commitments, covenants, and promises. People can also be united in spirit and in the flesh. What does it all mean? We have an active set of cords that are tied to our internal set of agreements. Yes! Our agreements produce exposure to dreams at a minimum, and firm agreements produce firm cords that connect us to a dream life.

Here are some common cords of agreement that are tied to our dream life:

- **Any forms of agreements**
  - What you like, what you love, what you surround yourself with, etc.

- **Agreements with fears**
  - Fear of failure, not being good enough, confidence, fear of lack, etc.

- **The unconscious, preconscious, conscious state**
  - Thoughts that your mind is producing

- **Agreements about who you are or who you are not**
  - Preconceived ideas about who you are, and who you have identified to be

- **Any forms of covenants**
  - Commitments and Covenants that you have agreed to. Who you're married to, friends with

- **Soul ties**
  - Past and present relationships, especially those involving intimacy

- **Agreements in proximity**
  - You live in a certain city, neighborhood, region, or country

In addition to our cords of agreement, we have an ultimate cord that ties us to our divine and true purpose. It's called the silver cord, spoken about in the Bible. This connects our spirit to God and our true purpose. This cord operates exactly as an umbilical cord would operate. The umbilical cord is a lifeline connection, but the mother and child are two completely different people. The umbilical cord does lots of things, but one of its primary tasks is that it carries blood from the mother to the fetus's heart!

In the connection of the mother and baby, the baby can feel the heartbeat of the mother and get vital nutrition sent straight to all the essential areas for development. This happens when the baby is sleeping and awake. Yep. All the time. Does it stop? The process only stops when the umbilical cord is broken, when the baby reaches full term, or, in historical times, it is 40 weeks. The cord is broken because its purpose is complete.

The same goes for us with the silver cord. We are served vital information every day, and oftentimes when we sleep. We receive just like a downloaded message in our email inbox. We have this connection as long as we are alive. The silver cord is tied to the cycle of our life. It is broken when we die. Now we know where dreams come from. I know it's pretty expansive, given the nature of agreements, but it's essential to see how we can set up our dream life and guide it with our alignments, lifestyle, thoughts, and emotions.

The examples of cords of agreement in dreams are genuinely endless. Nevertheless, here are a few:

Maria goes to bed and has a dream about marshmallows. She see some marshmallows in her dreams in various ways. After she woke up, she thought that was weird. However, she has a sweet tooth. She was craving something sweet. After her sweet tooth was satisfied, the craving went away. Her body was telling her something that she wanted.

James has a fear of driving. He often dreams about terrible things when he gets into a car. The scenarios are endless. Every time he gets into a car, something bad happens in his dreams. His fear drives this dream.

The unconscious state often provides us with leftover dreams. Jane loves to watch action movies late at night. Sometimes she has dreams about things that are inside those movies. This would be an unconscious, preconscious, conscious dreaming cycle. Her mind is filled with ideas as it goes into deep sleep. What she sees in her dreams, in this case, is directly attributed to her cognitive state.

Married couples often have dreams about each other. Their commitments and covenants are tied to each other. Tom has dreams about his wife's heart. He dreams about the things that she wants and needs. Sometimes these dreams are realistic, and sometimes they are unrealistic in his mind. Tom gets these dreams because of his commitments to his wife. He is connected to her in various ways, including his dream life. Because of this connection, he is provided with an extra layer of communication based on his cords of agreement with her. Now, he gets the wonderful opportunity to consider ways that he could connect, improve, and grow in his relationship with his wife.

## Thoughts + desires + personal agreement = New Cords

A married woman with several kids, not too happy about her marriage, starts talking to another guy. One night, she has a dream about sleeping with him and having a child with him. She wakes up and feels like this is something God has called her to do. She leaves her husband of 20+ years and ends up having a child with the new guy. I would initially say this was a dream based on personal agreement. Thoughts produce desires, and the agreement produced a warning dream on the new cord that was established. The warning dream was interpreted as a confirmation and not a "this will happen if you don't stop what you're doing" warning dream. You may also call these new cords "heart strings" as they pull on our hearts to consider the path of our thoughts and desires.

New cords of agreement can be established or reinforced daily in our lives. We need to know this. If you do a self-assessment on the cords of agreement you have today, it may change next year. Our dream language will morph and change based on your cords of agreement. Finding out where your dreams come from is half the understanding necessary to interpret your dreams. This chapter is vital in our approach to the beginning of interpreting our dreams. Take a self-inventory of your cords of agreement and see what you find. You may discover that specific fears are directly tied to the dreams that you're having. Or you may discover that particular desires and hopes feed the dreams you encounter. This self-inventory process should happen regularly. Anytime you feel like your dreams are changing, you should take inventory of your life, influences, and situations.

# THE STUDY

Currently, over 7,100 languages are being spoken in the world today. Each language has a foundation of thought that ties in images, lines, circles, and repeatable custom icons. Every language has a different origin story; some share the same fundamentals and nuances. Dating back to around 3000 BC, artifacts were found with some of the world's earliest writing tablets. Even one of the world's first customer complaints was written on some stone by the Samaritans.

In all of the 7,100 languages, which one is right? Is there one that is superior, closer to perfection than any other? Who knows? Even more important than one being better than the others is the fact that groups of people got together and started to adopt a common understanding of the images, lines, circles, and repeatable icons. Of course, some languages are more comprehensive than others. In Papua New Guinea alone, there are over 800 languages spoken. Humans have been very malleable over the centuries in learning and adapting to these new languages.

Your language is the one you know. It's the one you expect. It's the framework for how you communicate and understand. Consider for a moment a neighboring country that speaks a different language? Is it wrong? No, absolutely not. They are just different for various reasons. Where they come from? Their past influences, etc. And if you really want to learn about who they are and understand them better, you may need to learn their language. If not, you are stuck guessing what their symbols mean, and icons say.

In the midst of 7,100 languages, there is a language we can all understand. It's a language that has the singular focus of providing us with vignettes to enlighten us into our purpose. It's truly a divine language because it is so inherently tied to us and because everyone on the earth has access to it. Welcome to the dream language. A user-based and developed language of symbols, icons, and vignettes. This language has been around longer than time. It is built into who we are and can be formed by us at the same time. I cannot wait to share this language with you!

This divine language is actually the first language in the world. It helped shape the world that we know and love today. Even God has used dream language before the foundations of time. He hoped and planned before He ever created anything. I want to take you into a few rooms back in the Dream House to show you how your dream language can be formed. You will see how it's like vignettes (small episodes, small illustrations, or pictures). I like the word vignette because of its meaning, from the vine, and when we get vignettes, we are connected to the source.

## Study

In order to truly unlock our understanding of the dream language, we first need to explore the study in the Dream House. Have you ever seen a centuries-old door with ancient carvings? My study has one of the most beautifully carved doors. It has intriguing designs that all mean something, with mural-style carvings coated with time. The door itself has a thousand stories to share, and each one wants to talk to me at the same time.

With a few fingers, I push the door open. I can see one singular light coming from the right ceiling and wall. It is perfectly lit, yet fairly dark. As I look down, I read the words "Wisdom of the Age," which can be seen on the floor mosaic in between the acacia wood floors. The floors creaked when I walked in until I stepped onto a tapestry rug, a composite of my life's story woven in muted fabrics. On top of the tapestry is one of the room's inspirations, a beautiful huge globe that takes up the center of the room. It may have been ten feet around.

The study has a desk over on the right side, just under the double-decker library wall, and a spiral staircase with a balcony. There are books filling the shelves from floor to ceiling. So many books, some of them are in paper bags against the wall. I am always drawn to two particular bags of books next to my desk and one next to the door. Those are books that I feel like I am to write. They are old vintage books, but the words are timeless, so they will carry on.

Over my desk is a Venetian-style chandelier reflecting the candlelight or the stained glass window on my right. This is the room where I go to study and learn. I go to it to read and be instructed. Anytime I desire to learn something, I walk into this room. It holds the "wisdom of the ages" inside.

Every book seems to have a universe inside. There is one book that sits on my desk on the right-hand side. It's called the story of my life. I open it up and write in it often. When the book is open, my words are depicted inside a shape in a phenomenal way back into the visual memories right on the pages. It's like watching real-life vignettes inside every word. Some clips have more color than others, based on what I was reading. Everything seems to be talking to me to help me learn more about myself and record who I am today.

Another book that I have on my desk is called My Dream Language. When I open up this book, I can see inside myself. It is a weird, fascinating feeling. It is written with one voice, and each chapter title is a symbol. There are many, many symbols. More than is possible to count. The table of contents says one word, "Signified." Which means sign, point to, mark, or idea expressed by a sign. Some chapters have a symbol and no text, just a picture. The book was not written in my native language at first. It was written in symbols first. When I hold this book, I feel the vibrations of the moment. It's like being in a train station when the train goes by. Overwhelmed in a good way, with every physical sense being maximized.

I grab the book and consider a dream. I am led to open up My Dream Language book, and the symbols start jumping off the pages. I see a thousand intended stories, lessons, and meanings wrapped up in one icon. On every page, a thousand new stories, lessons, and meanings. Once I focus on the symbol, I can see the thousand meanings all at once, and then I start to rightly divide what I see to help me unlock my dream.

## Dream Messengers

In my dream language book, there are messengers that help me. One messenger or many messengers get assigned to deliver a dream and host it. They hold the key to understanding the dream. A symbol is one of the main messengers. A symbol is a fantastic builder, and he knows exactly how to host a dream and help me walk along to my purpose. The messengers are like an icon on my phone or computer. They host the dream just like an icon hosts the folders and windows to look through. I can see so many new options when I click on that icon. The applications on my phone or computer operate in the same way as with symbols and other messengers. Once you see something in a dream, there might be an entire world of possibilities hidden behind it. This doesn't make dream interpretation harder; it makes it come alive.

Let us define symbols and the other dream messengers to know more about key elements that we will find in our dreams. I really want to emphasize symbols for you in this chapter, but I cannot miss an awesome opportunity to be a little comprehensive for those that seek even greater context for the kind of speech we get in dreams. Perhaps you will see in these quick definitions some dream elements that you have encountered and didn't even know it. We will review the types of dreams in a later section. Right now, let's review how dreams come to us. What is the primary mode of delivery? And is it through a symbol, image, riddle, etc.?

## Dream Messengers and Dream Language Lexicon

These words will help develop your understanding of what your dream language is. This is going to be how you enter this world of dreams or how they are delivered to you. Let's look at each one of these words and their definitions, keeping this as a reference for you to begin to understand the different ways and types of your dream language. When we're looking at dream language, we are going to look at different ways things can be interpreted.

### Signified
To be a sign, to point to, to represent something else.

### Symbol
A representation of something else. An Icon or window of understanding that points to something greater. For example, the icons on a desktop computer open up greater possibilities once

the icon is clicked on.

## Jargon

A word or phrase that is not formal or literary, typically one used in ordinary or familiar conversation. The use of ordinary or familiar words or phrases. "The colloquialisms of the streets." For example, I wasn't born yesterday. Put your money where your mouth is.

## Dialect

A dialect is a language spoken in the area you're from or a widely used saying that is figurative in meaning, different from the saying's literal meaning. Here's an example, "To bite off more than you can chew." This would mean that you tried to do something which is too difficult for you.

## Metaphor

A figure of speech in which a word or phrase is applied to an object or action to which it is not literally applicable. You see a car in a dream. A car in a dream represents your gifts, talents, and abilities. The dream might not be about the car. but your gifts, talents, and abilities. Your gifts, talents, and abilities also get you to where you want to be, just as a car does.

## Veiled Language

Some of our dreams seem to be telling us something that we aren't able to see or understand. Veiled language is not openly shown or stated. It's not expressed in a way that is clear and direct, it's hidden, and you have to learn how to see it.

## Non Sequitur

A conclusion or a statement that does not logically follow the previous argument or statement. Dreams sometimes seem to have these vignettes that go from one to another, and they don't seem to make any sense. However, a closer look often reveals that it's the same dream at a different location and from a different point of view. While you're learning your dream language, be on the lookout for these types of dreams. Other times, it could be a different dream altogether. So remember the learning curve you're on and be patient with yourself. This language can be difficult at first.

## Paradox

A seemingly absurd or self-contradictory statement or proposition that, when investigated or explained, may prove to be well founded or true. For example, a person that stops going to work but makes more money from their business. You may have a dream like this and find it hard to believe. It does seem unreasonable or illogical, but sometimes the workers can get more done when the boss isn't in the room looking over their shoulder micromanaging everything that's being done.

## Caricature

A picture, description, or imitation of a person in which certain striking characteristics are exaggerated in order to create a comic or grotesque effect. When you have these types of dreams, look at what's being exaggerated, and you will find out the meaning of the dream. When you have a dream, and you have a very big nose, this dream could tell you that you have great discernment. With your nose, you can tell if the food is good or bad.

## Implied language

It is suggested but not directly expressed; implicit. This is a big part of dream language. Look for clues that are hidden between the lines or concealed. Suggested but not directly expressed. Look at what's understated, exaggerated, or blown out of proportion for better or worse than in reality.

### Dark Speech

A statement or image has to be searched out in order to be discovered. This is a big part of dream language! Dreams that give you a deep desire to know the interpretation often have a lot more to say to you during the journey of understanding the meaning of the dream than the dream itself. This is a big part of dream life.

### Allegory

A story or picture that you can interpret and find a hidden meaning. The story of Jonah and the whale, in the Bible, represents Jesus' death and resurrection. Jonah was three days and three nights in the belly of the whale, so the Son of Man was three days and three nights in the heart of the earth.

### Literal

Not exaggerating or being metaphorical, but plainly stated, and able to be perceived easily. These types of dreams are actually most often visions. The night visions will usually be fulfilled in the next few days. The vignette will play out just as you saw it in the night vision. It will literally happen. You may be the type who has literal night visions 80%of the time, and the other 20%, has dreams. This is a rare gift.

## Where did you come from?

So you had a dream, and the messenger brought you a bunch of symbols to interpret. One of the first questions you should consider is where did this messenger come from? We learned how dreams are formed in the previous chapters and how they set up new cords based on forms of agreement that we have. In the same way, dreams are formed similar to where dreams are sourced. This is very important to know because identifying where your dream comes from is half of your interpretation. Did your dream come from your spirit, soul, body, emotions, pizza, or God?

Let us review a few dream origins so you can identify where the messengers are coming from.

- **Divine purpose**
  - Can come from any origin or any angle. All dreams stem from the protraction of our divine purpose. They work for or against our purpose. Our divine purpose is vast. It can be something small or very expansive as it connects to our life.
  - Please see the divine purpose section in the chapter one for a full definition

Some common cords of the agreement you will see in divine purpose are:
  - Proximity: You are living in a certain city, your neighborhood, region, or country.
  - People: Learning about your past, present, and future connection to people.
  - Self-defining: Truth establishing dreams, mindsets, learning about yourself, your gifts, skills, and thoughts.
  - Situations: Unlocking the nuggets of truth and lessons from the past or providing a glimpse into the future

- **Demonic**
  - The juxtaposition of having a divine purpose. We can be lost, tormented, oppressed, or mistreated. You get the idea. The origin of these dreams can be very dark and taxing to wake up from. They are often immersive, intrusive, and alarming and ultimately lead us away from our divine purpose. Not all dark dreams are demonic. Remember, it's not the messenger; it's the origin.

- **Emotions**
  - All 66 emotions (see Jeremy and Dr. Ally Butrous at drallybutrous.com on that resource) can be the originator of our dreams.
  - Sadness, fear (any fear), pleasure, joy, contentment, anger, etc. A huge source of many of our dreams is pointing out our emotional state.
  - Our thoughts from our unconscious, preconscious, and conscious s state of mind
  - Thinking about not finishing laundry before bed can produce dreams about overwhelming laundry. Also, thinking about a problem at work can produce dreams that help solve the problem.

- **Spirit**
  - Our spirit is the source of many of the dreams that tie us into our ultimate purpose in life. It helps us avoid huge mistakes and speaks to us in monumental ways.

- **Soul**
  - Our soul is the source of updates from ourselves, our connections, relationships, and past relationships, especially those involving intimacy.

- **Body**
  - Our body is the source of dreams directly connected to our body. Is there a problem somewhere? Are you getting a hormone surge and your body is trying to tell you something? Did you have physical trauma, and your body is not done processing this? Is your body telling you that you have a sex drive? Is your body trying to let you know about a health issue?

- **Garbage Pizza**
  - There's no rhyme, no reason, no connection to our

purpose, and no application to derive from the dream. It's a mess, and it can be trashed when a dream is identified as a garbage pizza dream. The best thing to do is throw it away and forget about it.

These messengers come packed with what I like to say universal application. See, if the dream was only for one moment in time, what is its use tomorrow, or in five years? Our dream life is tied to our divine purpose. Therefore, the dreams we have will mostly be packaged in a way for us to get something from them throughout our life. The divine purpose dreams are the ones that you want to keep and refer to. These dreams last forever. The dreams that do expire are for warning and instruction. They do have value and should be used to develop your dream vocabulary, but they are limited to a specific period of time in relation to the dream. Divine purpose dreams have no limited period of time.

If we were to get a short-term message in a dream that is predefined (e.g. go here, say this) how much more individual participation is in that? A little? Dreams are so much more than directives. Later in the book, we will define dreams that reveal what is in us versus dreams that are getting us to act. The study is the room I return to every time I am learning something. There are books on people, numbers, things, and books on others' dreams. I can learn from others' dreams. As a matter of fact, there are clues inside others' dreams that help me learn about myself. Why? The source of our divine purpose is the same. We are all human. I can learn from dreams of old, biblical dreams, and my neighbor's dreams. This all takes place in the study.

Developing your dream language takes time. Studying the dream language lexicon does help to provide the context for how dreams are given to us. What vehicles are they in? Is my dream veiled speech symbolic, literal, or signified? These are questions that will provide us with the quick response foundation to begin to interpret our dreams.

## Studying leads us to learn about ourselves.

As we continue to study the dream origins, we will find out more about ourselves. We will see the power of divine purpose and how it feeds our dream life and the elements that are connected to it. We will see the various forms of emotions that we have on a daily basis that feed our dreams. This will be a self-discovery of all the emotions that we have. It will be a fantastic study because I've never considered having these kinds of emotions before, but I realize that our dreams tell us things about ourselves.

Is your body telling you something that you need to know? Are you getting dreams better from the spirit or the soul? How about having a pizza dream? Because you know where the origin of dreams is, now you can start to properly understand where your dreams are fueled from and where they're taking you.

# PERCEPTION

When I was a kid, they sold these pictures at the mall that if you looked at for a while, your eyes would adjust, and you would be able to see an incredible image in 3-D pop out! But at first glance, you could see nothing. You had to train your eye how to see the hidden image. Some of my friends could never see what was hidden inside the picture. They weren't patient enough to spend the time to train themselves, but once you could see it, you couldn't unsee it! Learning a dream language in the beginning looks flat like a simple drawing, but as you learn this language, the dream takes on another dimension, which is amazing. It's like a whole new world opens up for you.

## Do you value what you see?

Building out your dream language is establishing relatable, valuable meanings and perceptions of a person, place, or thing. This points to that. This thing means that. This thing opens up this door of thought. Through this chapter we will look at some core elements that help shape our perception of ourselves, our dreams, and those around us. We will shy away from any action-related matters, and develop some ways we look at things and why.

We can get a significant understanding of our dreams and others by honoring our dreams. I believe deeply that honoring your dreams and what they are saying is key to having more dreams. I care about the message, and the more I care, the more I dream. Some of you may think poorly of yourself. You beat yourself up with your thoughts and words all the time. That needs to change because you are valuable and worth more than you think. Also, as your thoughts improve about yourself, your dream life will go with it. If you have a low self-worth image, you will not care very much about what you see in your dreams. See how this is all connected to you?

As we begin to place a "value" and "honor" on what is signified and symbolic in our dreams, we will build fundamental blocks of agreement and understanding with ourselves. We are essentially telling ourselves that this language, no matter how foreign, is important, and I am open to learning and growing in it. This "value" and "honor" is a composite of attentive listening in order to learn and extract the message that the signified is telling us.

As I approach my dreams and their contents, my heart and mind need to carry a basic care and value for what my dreams are saying. I like to tell myself, "Ok dream; I am open to hearing you out." That is a fundamental value, therefore, I am giving a place in my heart and mind to have more dreams and go deeper in their understanding. The exact value you should have for your dreams as a whole should trickle down into the elements of the dream. I have a question for you. It is a rhetorical one. Do you have people you care more about than others in your life? Of course, you do. The same values are applied to our dreams. Do you have objects in your life that you care more about than others? Absolutely! This also carries over into our dreams.

We set values based on our thoughts, understandings, feelings, experiences, spiritual influences, and societal norms, to name a few.

At a minimum, you should get to know yourself enough so you can take inventory of these things. If you don't have a basic assessment of your thought life, mindsets, feelings, and past experiences, then how can you harness the images that come to you in a dream? And to know if they are important enough to focus on in a dream? Be encouraged by the road we are building together. Look ahead for the opportunity you have to get to know yourself better today and now! If you have never considered taking an inventory of yourself, you should start today and perhaps speak with a life coach to help you.

## What are you bringing to shape your dream life?

The eye is a fascinating organ, the way it translates the world to us in detail and color. When we see something, that image is flipped upside-down and sent to a particular part of our brain for translation, association, and connection. Our eyes do not ultimately store our database of experiences, thoughts, and frames of reference. This example carries over into how we see and perceive in life and in our dreams.

What you see with your eyes is not exactly what you see in front of you. It's what your brain sees. You are taking pictures with your eyes, and your brain is translating these pictures into "what you see." Your perception is first and foremost formed in your mind. Remember, we sleep with our eyes closed. It is not about what we see but what we perceive. These perceptions are largely built on our framework, which we bring to our dream life.

As we have discussed, what we perceive in life spills over into our dreams. What do you value deeply? Animals? Vacation? Specialty coffee? Do you have a particular hobby that you love? Shopping? Gardening? Fishing? What do you spend your time doing the most? Watching TV? Which shows? Working? Teaching your children? Who do you take advice from? What podcasts do you listen to? Whose books do you read?

The world often shapes our thoughts and values around us. The people you listen to shape your perceptions about your own life and about your dream life. If you watch the news often, then you will think more like a news cycle and therefore dream like one, as well. You will encounter crises, drama, politics, happy stories, and news. If you listen to any kind of music, you will see that it affects your thoughts, current emotional state, and temperament. As our mood goes up and down, we too will see a reflection in our dreams and the way we perceive our dreams. Our dream content will change based on our perceptions, and normal dreams will be viewed and perceived in a particular way based on our moods, emotions, and perceptions. Everything is affected by our mindsets, moods, emotions, ideals, and value systems. This is what we bring into our dream world.

## Symbolic, signified, and literal

Let's evaluate a few keywords as we start to perceive dreams differently. A symbol is an isolated symbol. Symbolic is a process of serving as a symbol. Signified is the meaning or idea expressed by a sign, pointing to a sign, or a symbol. Literal is the process of evaluating things in their most basic sense without metaphor; it's strict and factual. We have discussed these words lightly in the previous chapters, and now they should become the home base for your dream world. When you propose questions about your dreams, it will be through the lease of these words.

## Literal

As we learned in the "study," dreams come to us in many forms, and 98% of the dreams we will get will be signified. The images, pictures, vignettes, clips, and expressions in the dream will point to something bigger, more meaningful, and expansive, as an icon on a computer or a window looking outside. The number 98% is based on historical, biblical, and personal calculations. That means less than 2% of your dreams should be taken 100% literally. Some seasons may change slightly, but they won't change too much because the goal of our dreams doesn't change. Therefore, the premise of signified dreams versus literal dreams will always remain the same.

There is a dream sequence I would like to mention quickly to add to this. I like to call this sequence, "You're plugged in." It is when you have a dream that is to be signified, but you have a timestamp placed in your dream to bring you present-day content. The dream is not to be taken 100% literally. It is a signified dream, but that doesn't mean it is all fiction. No, not at all. Signified is simply a sign pointing to something else.

Here is an example: James was traveling and asked himself if he should visit a monastery. Would it be worth the money to make a day trip to visit this place he saw online? That night he had a dream. A spiritual mother in his life, who had since passed away, showed up in the dream and asked him to show her around the monastery. He took her around and taught her about this beautiful place that she would have never been able to see in her life. He felt like he was letting people see places they would never be able to see if he went. He felt a sense of purpose and assignment in the dream. He knew he should go. He woke up from the dream and planned his trip for a few days later. Dream fulfilled!

In James' dream, he had a divine purpose attached to his spiritual mother and his feeling of showing people something special from his perspective. The dream was not "literal." It was signified.

Some elements were "real," but they pointed to a lifestyle of interpretation, not precisely " verbatim." This person that he cared about showed up in his dream. That provoked lots of beautiful emotions in him. He was connected to this honorary figure in his life, which connected him to his purpose in the dream. Obviously, she has since passed away, and she will not and did not physically show up to be with him at this Monastery. I know that may sound silly, but I need to emphasize the small differences between signified and 100% literal. This lens of signified embraces all of the tiny details. It holds true to the dream and doesn't let interpreters say it is black and white, right or wrong, fiction or truth. Those lines cannot be drawn in the dream world. Why not? Because you perceive the truth. Your perception creates the lines of what is good, meaningful, and accurate.

These truths are yours to create. That is ultimately why they are tied into your divine purpose. If not, you would be a bag floating around in the wind. They must be anchored somewhere. Those who do not have an anchor change their perceptions every day based on how they feel, and that produces unproductive lives and poor dream interpretation.

Even though most people think literal dreams are the standard, they are not. We don't use veiled speech in any form of our lives unless you're a director/screenwriter or poet. We talk plainly, to the point, and try to avoid confusion. That is how we get stuff done. Imagine people walking around the office, taking in veiled speech, parallels, and dark sayings? "Ben, the cloud over you will burst when the moon goes down. How light is your load to make it through the gate? When we transcend the hills of our expiration, we will walk into seven hills filled with bubblegum." HAHA Yeah! That's not going to help get any work done.

We don't talk like that, but sometimes our dreams do. Why? Because the dream could be a concentrated speech with a thousand intended meanings tied to your life purpose or many other reasons. See, if the dream was only for one moment in time, what is its use tomorrow, or in five years? Our dream life is tied to our life. The dreams we have and their application, meaning and timing will help us discover and develop our dream language and ultimately lead us to our divine purpose. Therefore, our dreams will mostly be packaged in a way for us to get something from them down the road of our life.

Why can't it just be black and white, right and wrong? Why the veiled messages, puzzles, and symbols? The short answer is the type of messenger you get in your dreams is calibrated to the type of dream you are having and what the message contains. Some dreams are designed to bother and provoke us, or confuse us into mystery, or bug us enough to get interested in seeking out meaning. See, our dreams are not butlers serving everything to us on a silver platter. They keep us on the right track. When receiving "you're plugged in" dreams, you dance with your dreams. Sometimes you lead the next step, and sometimes your dream leads. The feeling of this happening is you are at the right place, at the right time in your life, doing what you're supposed to be doing. It's a great feeling of satisfaction.

If we were to get a short-term message in a dream that is predefined (e.g. go here, say this) how much individual participation is in that? A little, or not much at all? Dreams are so much more than directives. It is actually quite silly to consider that part of our life should be on autopilot, while the other parts require our participation. In some beautiful way, signified dreams filled with symbols and colloquies bring us more user participation than any other type of speech. We are drawn into the mystery, the hunt, the intrigue. We dive into self-discovery, past recollection, and our perceptions about who we are and what we are about. Dreams can and often do impact every area of our life, and are not simply limited to getting something done quickly.

If dreams are geared to change us to become better versions of ourselves and guide us to our divine purpose, why would we settle for quick answers and only seek literal interpretations?

## 2% of the time

As I have stated, about 2% of our dreams are literal. Suppose you have a literal dream. You will know it to the core of who you are. It is clear as day with no veiled speech, and no messing around. The writing will be on the wall. Frequently, literal dreams are tied to a type of dream we will discuss later in the book called warnings. These dreams are like a 911 call, straight to the point, with no extra words or pictures included. They are to be as direct as possible and delivered in a way for you not to be mistaken in their interpretation, at all. That is the point of this type of dream.

A woman in Philadelphia had a dream one night that her daughter was going to harm herself using a rope. She dreamt of running downstairs to her and saving her from hanging herself. In the dream, she was given a very clear message to save her daughter. She woke up from the dream and thought a lot about it. She Googled the meaning of the words and considered the dream's meaning until she forgot about it. Later on that night, her daughter attempted suicide with the use of a rope downstairs. The message was clear, but not acted on. Her daughter survived the incident with some life-altering injuries. These types of dreams are very important and very serious.

Here is another example of a 100% real literal dream that was given to an author with clear instructions. This man wrote extensively and was in the middle of several books. He went to bed one night, and out of the sky, he caught his next book. He could see the picture on the cover and all the chapters that went inside. It was perfectly packaged for writing the next day. His entire book was given to him in a dream. Wow! There are so many other stories like this one from inventors, authors, singers, and creators. Dreams like this help us see a very plain script to go and create.

This section was first in the chapter because so many get stuck on a literal interpretation of everything. This is the way they see life and, therefore, it is the way they see their dreams. With what we know now, 98% of dreams would be misinterpreted if a literal lens was applied to our dreams. That doesn't discount the importance of a literal dream, nor the real 100% factual elements of the dream that are signified or symbolic. We need to see dreaming as a holistic sequence of elements. We cannot simply have one lens for everything in life, literal or not, symbolic or not, correct or wrong, true or false. That is not how we should operate and, therefore, not how our dreams operate.

## Symbols are windows and doors.

I return to my Dream House study every time I am learning something. Do you see how in my mentioning of the study, I am connected to a whole host of avenues of thought that we have previously established? Where in the study am I standing? What am I looking at? What am I doing? That is exactly how symbols work. They open up doors or windows into a world of possibility. We create these symbols and also learn about them along the way. Symbols are like the ABC's of dream language. It's the beginning of learning how to speak, read, and write the language of dreams. I am born into a world of dreamers, and this is a very good thing for me.

See, there are books on people, numbers, and things in my study. They are all here to help me in my own dream world. There are even books on others' dreams. I can 100% learn from anyone and everyone's dreams. As a matter of fact, there are clues inside others' dreams that can help me learn about myself. Why? The source of our divine purpose is the same. We are all human. I can learn from dreams of old, biblical dreams, and my neighbors' dreams. They are all beneficial to me in establishing my own dream language. I will continue to tie in dreams from everywhere to show you how we can learn from every kind of dream.

Let's start with an easy one. A pen, for the sake of this illustration. The pen is a real pen with no fancy stuff shooting out of the ink holder or cryptic messages, this time. There is a pen all by itself in the vast nothingness. What do you think of this pen? What does it point to? What does it help you remember? What does this pen create emotionally for you? The pen is simply a thing, but it could have so much meaning depending on who it is shown to.

I see organization in the pen because I always have one with me to help me stay organized. I see readiness because I always take notes. I see contracts because pens are always used for contracts. I see inspiration because the written word always inspires me. That is what I see with this pen floating around in the void of nothingness. Do you think your neighbor thinks exactly the same way you do when they see the pen? Probably not. Until you are really good at interpreting your own dreams, you should shy away from the direct interpretation of someone else's. It would be best to see for yourself before you can guide someone else.

Let's consider another element. Your father is now holding the pen. For some, you may see participation with your birth father. Some may see their dreams taken away because they don't know their father or had a bad relationship with him. Some would say this dream is garbage because their dad had never used a pen in his life. Do you see the vast application we can apply to something so simple? We all see and perceive the way we are.

These symbols are a composition of who we think we are. What we have been through, our past, our family history, what we believe, and our culture. There are so many things that form our perceptions. We don't need to learn them in this book, but simply know that there are many elements that contribute to them. Each and every person will have their own personal dream language. It is custom and beautiful that way. Dream language is as unique as our fingerprints; no two are alike!

Whenever we encounter a symbol, it opens up a door or window of understanding for us. The emphasis is on learning. It's like learning a new letter in the alphabet of your dream. The vast majority of symbols we're looking for in our dreams aren't necessarily for an application. They are for education. It's the very beginning step of understanding dream language. If you're always looking for what you need to do right away in your dreams, you are missing the main point of dreaming, to better know yourself.

Sometimes it's not about the "pen" at all. The "pen" just got you thinking, feeling, remembering. It's an icon to let you into a mindset or a series of thoughts. That's what I would call a transitional object instead of a destination object. A transitional object is pointing to something else, and a destination object is the goal. Think of the street sign on your way to your friend's house. The street sign is not your goal, but it points you in the right direction. Your friend's house is the goal.

## Looking for what is hidden

As we dream and interpret our dreams, we find ourselves in new places after the dream is finished. We don't know where we are going all of the time when we dream, and therefore, the hidden parts of the dream are sometimes our destination. We want to search for what is hidden because it will lead us to our destination. For example, if you're in a foreign country and being told something in a language you don't understand. This foreign language to you, is what is hidden. Inside the language is your key to getting to where you need to go. You may not know this language, but it is essential to find your next clue.

When we see a symbol or symbols, like "your father holding a pen," think of it as a letter written in code that you must convert into "normal language." We have all heard the saying "read between the lines" or "read the white." It's what is being implied without being stated. What implied understandings are being shown to you? What thoughts and feelings did you recall? This is just the beginning to a more thorough process we will review later on in the book. These messages are veiled for your discovery and pursuit. The more work that's put into uncovering what a dream or symbol is, correlates to working on yourself. The more you work at it, the easier it becomes.

Have you ever been to the eye doctor? When you get a classic eye test to see if you need glasses or contacts, you see things with different magnifications. Perhaps a letter or icon is shown to you with different "powers" or "strengths." In order to see them clearly, you need to have a certain amount of concentrated focus on the letter or icon. When you have the correct "power," the image becomes perfectly clear when it may not have been visible beforehand. The lesson here is that we can see these elements in our dreams if we look for what is hidden and focus on the right things.

## What do they represent in your dream?

So your best friend shows up in one of your dreams. Yes, they are a real person. We know in life you do real things with them. However, in your dream life, they are a representative. Consider them as a representative of something versus the actual person. Let's discuss this a bit. When Ginny, my wife, shows up in one of my dreams I know she is my wife during the day, but at night she becomes a signified expression of my hopes, dreams, fears, and so much more. She is a means to speak to me about what I think she stands for. She has an influence on me that I have given her in our relationship. Therefore, she is able to speak to me about things that I don't talk to others about. When I think about her, I think about her love, care, our intimacy, our family, the deep parts of my heart, and our resounding love and connection, to say a few.

In my dreams, she can show up and embody any one of these things. She represents a message to me that I should pick up. Why was she in my dream? There is a specific reason, and the reason is not so that I can tell her I had a dream about her. It is fun to share and discuss your dreams when someone occurs in them, but that is not the main point of the dream. Very few dreams are for a literal translation, and therefore, very few dreams are for direct application with those that are in them.

*Here is a dream example: I walked into the house late after seeing an old friend. Ginny walks into the kitchen when I get home and says, "I made you dinner, but you need to learn about the ingredients in order to eat your dinner." I said, "Okay, where do we start?" She says, "You will need to learn fast, or you're going to starve. It's going to get cold, and then it will get moldy if you don't eat fast." I start frantically Googling each ingredient so I know exactly what it is, and then I finally feel like it is possible to eat. After I learn about each ingredient, I can take a bite.*

When I see Ginny in my dream, I see myself. I see my thoughts about her, my perceptions, my fears. I am learning about myself. In my dream, I exchange scenarios with Ginny in which I sort my emotions, plans, and desires. My dream example was not a literal dream. It was signified. I was reminded of who I was because of my past connections. The time element associated with my old friend and missing dinner created a connection emotionally for me. I didn't want to miss dinner, and that was apparent to me. Also, I do everything with Ginny so being apart is sometimes an indicator of something being off. In addition to feeling off, I realized I felt pressure to cram and perform if I did not know everything or all of the ingredients. This stressed me out, and I felt reassurance when I learned more. I would eat and feel accomplished and refreshed and made whole. Ginny (the real person) was a participant in that mindset with me. Her presence was significant to know what we could do together mentally, emotionally, and in life. However, her actually making me food and keeping me from eating with those crazy scenarios that played out in the dream would never happen. She is much nicer in person.

Every person can become a representative in this same way. Ask yourself, what do they represent and stand for? Guard your mind against the all-or-nothing conclusions. What do you have to learn and get from this person? Don't hesitate to consider their emotion, mindsets, geographical proximity, commonalities, the discrepancy from normal behavior, who you wish them to be, and of course, who they actually are to you.

## Where are you?

Have you ever had a dream that you're flying, talking to someone really close, hovering over the ceiling listening to a conversation, or trapped behind something? Your orientation inside your dream is paramount to your initial assessment of how to approach your dream. As we define and build more dream language, we are starting to think more comprehensively about our dreams and not so glibly. Instead of you thinking I was in a dream last night, where were you in the dream last night? What was your perspective? First, second, or third person point of view should all be considered in every dream.

Have you had a dream, and you weren't in it? That is important to note, as well. When you are absent it says just as much as when you're there, in some dreams. Everything means something in a dream until it doesn't. If you are flying in your dream, don't you think your perspective should align with that which is flying, high above, in the clouds, looking down? This is very different from looking at someone face to face with your noses almost touching. That perspective is eye to eye, perhaps intimate, confrontational, or possibly from a peer relationship. There is so much to glean from the first person's orientation in a dream.

## How do you see vivid colors or dull colors?

All of the details matter when you dream. How clear is the dream coming through? Is it coming over in vivid color or diluted, blurry, or in black and white? These are all perspectives and moods to enhance certain elements of the dream and blur out the non-important parts. The visibility is a story in itself as to what we should take away from the dream. Black and white dreams, for some, bring nostalgia; for others, the muted dreams speak to numb emotions. Collideascope dreams speak to a multitude of perspectives and options. Every color has meaning and sometimes personal attachment. We will look at specific colors and visuals later on in the book. Ask yourself why you see things this way. What is the purpose?

**Your dreams will lead you to your truth, but not always divine truth.**

Four people circle around an object, a knife. One looks at the knife and sees employment because they are a chef and use knives like that one every day. They are filled with optimism and excitement for what they love to do. The second person sees the knife, and they see a weapon. They have read many articles about knife fights in Japan. They are stoked with fear and anger. The third person sees a knife, and they have one similar to it at home that opens up beer. They love having people over, so it brings emotions of joy and relaxation. The fourth is reminded of a person they hate who used to cook for them. They are filled with disdain and bitterness when they see the knife. Who is correct in this example? Which one is true?

The answer is they are all true, and their personal truths provoked vastly different emotions. Each person is an individual and sees things their way. This doesn't make them concretely right or wrong, true or false. In this example, no one perspective was absolutely wrong based on one person's right to have their own thoughts. What if one of the people used their knife for gardening? Would that be wrong? Maybe not the best use of the knife, but perhaps it could be good. What about hurting someone? Would it be okay if it was in self-defense?

It is important to see that our personal truth at the moment is vast, quick to change, and very different from our neighbors. This should bring us a bit of caution as we consider the dreams of others and their interpretations of ours. Also, this sliding scale of truth should be understood on a divine scale in addition to our personal truth. One should be able to work diligently to differentiate their personal truth from absolute truth and our divine truth, which is built in our divine purpose. The absolute truth is like the sun coming up in the morning. It happens every day regardless of what we think it might do. The president of the USA's term limits can be two full four-year terms, if voted in twice. Fish swim in the ocean. These are absolute truths unless the facts change. Today, they are absolutely true; no debate on the facts.

We also have our divine truth, which is tied to our purpose. It encompasses our value systems, our morality, and our convictions. We relate to this as our truth or what we believe to be true. Do you see how vast our truth umbrellas can reach? The more our personal truths align with our divine truths our dream lives will be easier to understand. We will have fewer contradictions and confusion.

Our dreams pull us through thousands of options in our minds and hearts every day, slowly trying to guide us to our divine truth. However, we will often see and uncover our relative personal truth in many of these dream settings, and we need to be sober-minded in this. Our assessment of truths can be a manifestation of an emotion that we are having.

In a dream, you see yourself doing and saying things that you would never consider doing. You might be acting in a way that would be a shame if you did that during the day. A large majority of the time, this is not a "truth" indicator of who you are. Personal truth, absolute truth, and divine truth are often very different things. It's easy to reference dreams when we are naked. Imagine being naked in the middle of the street, in a dream. You walk around to all of your friends' houses and stand outside naked until they see you. Then you have completed the dream. Well then, the literal truth is that you would be breaking the law in almost every country on the earth, if you did that during the day.

However, in our dreams, we may see a vast number of truths present themselves to us so we can learn about our current state, or where we should be going. Perhaps, an accurate translation to this is it's time to be transparent with your friends until they actually see you without any disguises on. What if one of your friends in the dream doesn't want the transparent you? They only want a fake version of you. Perhaps, the dream is letting you in on your thoughts or the reality of your friend's thoughts about you. These are all important "truths" to consider.

Don't be so quick to frame something "true or false." There are many truths, and not all of them are good.

## What is up is sometimes down!

Dreams are not bound by the same laws of our waking life. Dreams are bound by the possibilities of our imagination trying to find a way to express what is being processed. The laws of nature do not apply to our dreams all the time. Sometimes, we turn into weird things in our dreams. Sometimes, those things do unnatural things like disappearing. I could name a thousand unnatural things that happen in dreams. That is why 98% of our dreams are not literal.

We should expect an unnatural experience, and then we will not be surprised when we get one. For instance, if we are flying in our dreams. Who doesn't want to go for another few flights the next time you sleep? If your words float around your head like a cartoon in your dreams, why not lean into it and find more ways to express those words in the next dream?

It is often difficult for our logical minds to wrap themselves around our dreams. We would generally say, "That did not happen; we were making it up, and let's be on with it." Our minds are designed to help us sort out the facts and make decisions. If we present a crazy mystical dream to our super-logical mind it will want to dismiss it, unless we lean into our dream and explore all of the pieces that are new, profound, and different. There is a creative center in our brain that loves when we explore the new and different.

Remember, a large majority of our dreams are for educational purposes only. When you watch a movie, you are generally not looking for action items and a to-do list. Let's see our dreams as theater, and entertain them as such if they get too crazy and wacky.

## Dreams are past, present, and future.

Time is the one thing that defines our existence. We entered a time when we were born, and we only have so much of it until we die. Time is also a focal point in our dreams, but it is applied differently. If I were to show you an image that is tied to your purpose, what time would it be in? Today, yesterday, or tomorrow? All of the above is the answer. We dream about our past, present and future all at the same time. If you have a dream with your past, present, and future in it, this means you are a normal person with a healthy dream life. It may seem strange and disorienting, but this is the composition of who we are.

We have a past to sort out in our dreams. So much of what we think about is what has happened to us. We are often fixated on what we regret and the experiences we have had. We are often trying to work out the emotions that were produced in our past and the images of ourselves that we have made. Our dreams are anchored in our past, and we will always have elements of our past to orient us.

# Present

Our present-day life is the core focus of all of our dreams. We dream in real-time, and most of our dreams pertain to a 90-day cycle of our present moments. It may not seem like this is the case, but now you can start to analyze this personally and see the evidence for yourself. How do we know this? Simply put, it's based on the way dreams are composed, and the elements of how they are formed, produced, and guided. We can see that dreams are tied to us and our present day and current life seasons.

Just as there are four different seasons in a year, we, too, operate off of seasons. Sometimes, those go with the earth's four seasons, and there are seasons of relationships, seasons of transition, seasons of building, and seasons of healing. When life happens to us, or we happen to it, we enter into a new season, and it has its own expressions. This produces seasons and cycles of dreaming tied to our present day.

We change the way we value our dreams when we know how closely related they are to our "now" season. Most of our dreams are for today, about our day, and surrounded by people, places, and things that are tied to today. However, even though an emphasis can be about today doesn't mean the dream's virtues can't transcend into life lessons and high-water markers for the remainder of your life. As we value the present emphasis on our dreams, they will help us along, guide us, and serve our needs today.

# Future

Our divine purpose is the reason why we have dreams, and this stems from where we are going and who we can become. The future emphasis on our dreams is vital to pull us forward in our life when sometimes we feel unsure, stuck, or lost. We are guided by the hope of what could be in the days ahead. When we perceive our future in our dreams, we should feel a pull into the possibilities. If we perceive warnings, we should be thankful for the heads up to allow us to push through, overcome, and plan ahead. The perception of our future in our dreams can seem daunting, unfamiliar, and new. However, it is our future, and we should embrace it. The more we lean into the future elements of our dreams, the more certain we will feel about our current day.

# UNDERSTANDING YOUR DREAMS

The road map of our dreams is assessed in three different steps. Where we start, what we see along the way to help us, and where we are going. In the previous chapters, we have evaluated some of the basic understandings of how dreams come to us, where they come from, and why they exist. We will bring this understanding to the first element of our road map, which is where we start.

I feel it's essential to evaluate our dream understanding in a few different ways because we need to see all facets of our dreams. I also feel the need to present one more way to see your dreams for those who need another linear example. Thus, I present to you the road map of dreams.

## Where do we start on the dream journey?

We start your dream journey today. What are you made of today? It is a composite of you, the good, bad, and the fantastic. It's all you. Your emotions, mindsets, mood, and past experiences are all fully alive in your dreams today. If you were to go to bed right now and start dreaming, your most present self would show up and contribute to your dreams. This is the starting line for your dreaming today, and it will be the same for tomorrow. This is good for us to know and for us to understand.

Where you are today contributes to the different types of dreams you will have, how frequent, and what kind they are. If you are stuck in a season of life, you may have repeating dreams. If you need to put more emphasis on learning and searching for answers, you may have dreams that are faded and focused. If you are stressed and anxious in life, you may find more exaggerated emotions playing out in your dream life. The person you are today is the dreamer who shows up at night.

It's important to know that you have a role in your dream life and that you should take inventory of your situations, emotions, mindsets, and influences because they contribute to the way you see your dreams. This inventory can be as basic as being mindful of your current season, situations, relationships, and how they are affecting you. Also, you can go so far as to inventory things that are off or seem to bother you, and that will paint a picture, as well, if you see them in your dreams.

Who you are today is, and can be, a direct contributor to where you are going. This is the same as your destination or where you are going. Your destination is, by design, a composite of your gifts, talents, skill sets, abilities, desires, passions, callings, what you love to do, are born to do, what you were educated in, and what drives you during the day. This is also where we start today. Perhaps you have already developed some of these identifiable markers in your life. This is the beginning and continuation of your dream journey.

We need to get you down the road of your dreams. In order to do that, you need vision, identity, passion, and a calling. That is what dreams are for. They plant seeds of purpose in you to get you on your way to something good, lasting, and life-giving. They spark your heart, beliefs, and mindsets to care for something, someone, or for a cause to move you into action. They plant in our hearts the essentials to wake, love others, go and work to take care of others to live a full life. Desires are built in our dream life. If you desire something, it was probably birthed in your dreams.

# On the road

Most dreams talk to us in our current season of life (past 90-120 days) but are tied to the entirety of our life. When we are on the road in our dream journey, we will get different kinds of dreams to keep us on the road. We will receive instruction dreams, warning dreams, step-by-step dreams, flashbacks, or deja vu dreams.

# Instruction Dreams:

The great thing about instruction dreams is that they can warn us about something that we think is okay, but we should not do it. It may be a small amount or a very large amount of instruction. If you are married, it would be very beneficial to listen to your spouse's dreams. It could save you a lot of time, energy, and money. I've had many friends share instruction dreams with me that affect their marriage, and the more they pay attention, the better they turn out. I have personally been able to avoid a lot of different situations that would have been harmful to my family and me through these kinds of dreams.

Dream: A wasp landed on the ring finger of my left hand. I was sitting in a bathtub, so I dunked my hand under the water. When I lifted my hand out of the water, it was still perched on my finger, but it still hadn't stung me, so I flicked it off. It seems to be related to marriage, but I'm not sure what the dream is trying to say.. My reply, "Sounds like a relationship that before you get too involved, you're going to realize he's not the 'one,' and you'll walk away from it and you won't be hurt!" Wow. That makes sense. A few months later, I found out that my friend is dating this guy, and I remember her dream and that he was not the one for her. But she goes through the motions anyway and ends up getting hurt. We don't need to do this. We can learn from our dreams and save ourselves the heartache. If she had remembered this dream and the interpretation, she would have asked more questions and saved herself from this destructive relationship. This is a complex process to learn and it takes time. Always remember that the dreams you dream are meant to help you make better decisions.

## Warning Dreams:

Warnings dreams do just that. They warn us. They warn us not to do something, go somewhere, or connect with a particular person. They can warn us about anything. This is how most people dream at first. They get a dream that tells them very clearly not to do something. Not all warning dreams are literal. But the dream itself is to provide us with a good amount of caution and inquiry for us to really consider what action(s) should be taken. It's important to know that the dream messengers and the different kinds of dream language that are used can still provide us with warnings. You may get a dream that has veiled or symbolic speech, and that could still be a warning dream.

You could have a dream about not going over to a particular person's house, or about not driving in a particular direction on your road trip. These warning dreams are messengers to tell you something to pay attention to. You should consider their cautions and be mindful of their messages.

## Step-by-step Dreams:

These dreams give us practical steps of what to do in our short-term lives. More often than not, the dream is speaking to a 30-90-day window in our present daily lives. They may present themselves in various forms and various types of dreams. However, they are very practical, chronological, and linear. It's always nice and refreshing to get a step-by-step dream because the work is done for the dreamer.

The average step-by-step dream is something like this place: speak to this person, do this thing. At the end of the dream, you know that you have succeeded if you completed all of the steps.

## Flashback Dreams:

Flashback dreams are some of my favorites and are very much like a deja vu dream. It is where the dreamer believes inherently that they have already been to the place that they are seeing right now. Moreover, it's not that they have already been there, but it feels like they have already been at this moment in time. It's like traveling back to a place you have already seen and witnessed.

I have a friend who gets flashback dreams all the time. They go to new places, and they experience a flashback phenomenon. The realization at that moment is that they are exactly where they're supposed to be and feel connected to their purpose and calling. It doesn't validate the facts of the dream, but it validates you as the listener.

Dreams act as guardrails to keep us on the road to our purpose. Imagine having a dream about your favorite person in the world. You sit down with them and have a conversation. You wake up, your heart is warm, and you are more inclined to connect with them and follow them, make plans with them, and do life with them. This is the same feeling of what it is like to be led along on our journey.

What if the dream we have is an outlier? How would we truly know if a dream is meaningful and purposeful? The key to understanding is to hold the dream in the balance of our divine purpose, our commitments, and what we know to be true and wholesome in our lives. There are several questions I ask myself when assessing a dream value and place.

1. Does the dream fit into my divine purpose today or down the road?
2. Does the dream help me and or my family?
3. Does the dream help my thoughts, emotions, and actions?
4. Does the dream help me work through parts of my past?
5. Does the dream have redemptive values I can gain from it?
6. Does the dream help me materially today or in the foreseeable future?
7. Does the dream break any commitments or covenants I currently have?
8. Does the dream align with who I am and the other dreams I have?

If you see that a dream is an outlier and invites you to break your morals and commitments that you have made, then it should be evaluated. Should the dream be thrown away? Should the dream be evaluated because of an area where you need to work on your emotions and thoughts? Do you feel tempted in your dream to do something that doesn't align with your morals? We will begin to sort and evaluate our dreams and see what serves us best to fulfill our purpose today and tomorrow.

# OUTLIER DREAM AREAS

## Immoral thoughts, feelings, and actions:

Any dream that promotes thoughts, emotions, or actions that break away from your convictions, morals, and ideals would be an outlier. These kinds of dreams distract, dilute our purpose, and pull us away from our personal convictions. They often leave us with feelings of shame, regret, and sin. We may wake up feeling like we have something to hide from our spouse or close relationships.

## Sexualized dreams:

Any dream that is sexualized that does not provide you with life-giving thoughts and feelings that establish and build your covenants, commitments, and marriage should be evaluated. We are vulnerable when we dream, and sometimes we may have a dream about sex that we would not agree with in our normal life. We should go through the checklist of questions to see if it lines up with who we are and who we want to be. Then seek meditative prayer and discussions with your partner about your dream. It's best to address these dreams in the beginning when you start having them and work on anything that needs attention, including your thoughts and relationship.

## Feelings that go against what you believe:

These are dreams where you are breaking laws, breaking your faith, or going out of your way to harm others. In dreams, it's totally normal to omit or display very strong emotions. However, if your emotions cross the line in your dream and you know that it is not you, how you would act, nor even recognize yourself when evaluating the dream, then it was going against your beliefs.

## Past traumas:

When past traumas replay themselves in different ways in our dreams, we often see several variations of the same thing. Car accidents, sexual traumas, and verbal and physical abuses are some examples. Traumas can be complex, and their impact can be also. We can be affected physically, mentally, and emotionally, to say the least. We should definitely see trauma dreams as an outlier that needs our attention. Depending on the trauma, a therapist or a life coach may also be recommended.

## Hypothetical fears (what if dreams):

Monumental fears leading to dreams can be outliers kept in check. Examples of this would be simple fears exacerbated into life-altering outcomes. These kinds of dreams tend to leave us with total loss outcomes. For instance, always falling short, always losing, always missing, or always wrecking. Fear is a big talker in our dreams, and these outliers need help and attention if we are producing them. Fears are not something that are foreign to us. Don't be afraid of solving them and working through the known fears you may have.

## Garbage Pizza dreams:

You watch an action movie and then have a dream that night about being in an action movie scene, and you are trying to escape the same plot. Or, you spill popcorn on the sofa, and in your dream that night you are destroying the earth because you spill too much popcorn. These are garbage pizza dreams and should not be taken too seriously—time to throw them away. No questions asked. Just let it go and forget about it, and have a good laugh about it.

## Three categories to evaluate our outlier dreams.

Outlier dreams can be silly, revealing, and sometimes haunting. There are three areas to evaluate our outlier dreams to know what to do with them. Sometimes we need to forget them, and sometimes we need to act swiftly. When we know where the dream came from, we can then know what to do with it.

**1. Was this outlier dream demonically inspired and out of your control?**
Ask yourself, do you feel personally attached to the dream in any way? Do you feel you caused, contributed to, or own it? If you answered no to the preceding questions, then it was probably demonically inspired, and you're best to leave it alone. If your dreams persist past 40 days, then evaluate what contributors you may have that fuel these kinds of dreams.

**2. Do I feel a sense of ownership in any of the outlier dreams?**
Good! If you feel attached to any one of the outlier dreams, then that is a good start to recognize your sense of ownership. That is the beginning of making things better. Perhaps you may have some less-than-life-giving areas in your heart and mind that are leading to potential cords of agreement, and those are worth evaluating. It's more than normal to work on yourself and sort through your thoughts. It's time to work on the areas that need healing, mending, fixing, and nurturing. The dream road to our purpose allows us to work on perfecting ourselves as we continue on our journey.

### 3. Garbage Pizza Dream

Did you have a garbage pizza dream? You know what to do. Throw it away. You may also benefit if you cut back on the caffeine after 2pm and be more mindful of movies and shows that alarm you. Also, pay attention if you are eating certain foods or eating too late.

## Dreams are important until they're not.

When you have an outlier dream, ask yourself what personal ownership you have pertaining to the dream. If you have ownership of the dream and feel a sense of responsibility in your actions, thoughts, and emotions, then you may have some work to do. We are given dreams to help us down the road of our life. This is a filtering and sifting process to remove any obstacles in our mind, body, and emotions, to lead us down the road to fulfilling our purpose.

How can we fulfill our purpose if we get stuck, derailed, and down about our perceived problems? It will be challenging to see clearly, act upright, and love well if we don't work to become the best version of ourselves and tackle the day ahead. Our dreams will help us reveal areas we should work on and take ownership of. They teach us the deep parts of our mind, heart, and emotions. If we have outlier dreams about our past, perhaps we must work through our thoughts more and find closure. We may need to seek counsel, forgive people, and move on. If we have sexually charged dreams about other people, perhaps we need to change our thoughts, desires, and habits during the day. If we dream about fears that we have, then we need to see the solution to those fears during the day.

All dreams are not good. We need to train our thoughts on upright, good things that connect us to a more meaningful life to uphold our commitments, covenants, and agreements. Having outlier dreams does not make you a "bad" person, nor does it mean you have some internal flaw in your identity. We all have things we need to work on; that's why we have dreams to help us out. Suppose you feel tempted in your dream life to break away from your core values? It's probably time to talk to someone and sort through your thoughts and feelings. Get the help you need to stay strong and grow into who you want to be. If you clean up your thoughts and emotions, and sort through your past in a way that leads you on the road to health, I assure you that you will have a wonderful healthy dream life thereafter.

## Where are we going?

Our dreams will take us to purpose and meaning. So what does it mean to live with purpose? Simply put, it means that you know what you are doing. You have goals and are passionate about what you do. Instead of simply letting the days pass you by, you work with purpose to make the most of each day. When you live with a purpose, you are not just existing. Purpose is the reason for which something is done or created or for which something exists. You are putting reason and meaning into your life. That is what you are doing on the dream road.

When we see purpose and meaning in front of us, we start to live on purpose. Living on purpose happens when we apply ourselves to what gives us meaning, perhaps making us more significant. We start to affect the people, places, and things around us in a positive way. As we live with purpose, we begin to shape our identity, beliefs, and value systems to benefit us and the people around us. The goal of our dreams is to bring us to fulfill the desire in our hearts, satisfy our hopes, love well, and become the best version of ourselves to ourselves and to those around us.

# Relational Process of Dreaming

Have you ever walked up to a perfect stranger, handed them your house keys, and expected them to know where you live and which key goes to what door? Absolutely not! You have to share elements about your personal life before they start to go in the right direction. In essence, you are going with them. We give our keys away to a perfect stranger when we remove the relational process from our dream interpretation. You cannot separate yourself from your dreams, and you cannot separate yourself from your interpretation or application.

Your life is central to the dream's interpretation. If you remove yourself from your dream, then who carries the dream? The dream doesn't exist without you. I have seen thousands of people try to interpret dreams by removing themselves from the interpretation. Why would they do such a thing? I believe there are two primary reasons. First, they don't know any better. They are taking their dream, throwing spaghetti on the wall, and hoping for anything that sticks. Second, they have some areas in their life, heart, and mind that need to be worked on that were presented in the dream, but they would rather avoid doing so. This can happen innocently and unconsciously because who wants to go through the painful process of bettering yourself?

So you have a dream about speaking to your friend about a particular matter. And in that dream, they speak back to you in your language, the things that you love and appreciate. Imagine now that you go and try to get an interpretation without sharing any of those details. How is the interpreter going to be able to find out the heart of your dream without knowing the personal details about you? More often than not, they're going to be guessing based on the principles that they know or that they've experienced. But, if you are to interpret your own dream, you're fully aware of the things that you love and appreciate, and know about that specific matter that was brought up. Because of those facts, you are empowered to interpret your own dream.

## Symbols are to be signified.

The most common mistake people make when starting to interpret their dreams is they think they can use generic definitions from dream books of old or Google in an attempt to unlock their dream. Symbols don't mean anything until they already mean something to you. What do I mean by this? Do you have a framework of understanding what you see in your dreams? Do you know what the symbols and icons mean to you? Do you know what the vignettes are saying and what the symbols point to? If not, you should come to terms with yourself and start building up your library of understanding. This will provoke a lot of questions and self-discovery, so you will need to make up your mind. A few examples could be, what do you believe about your childhood home? Who do your parents represent to you in your dreams? Who do you think you are? If you don't know, who will?

It's easy to pick up a dream dictionary and start guessing. However, what if you guess wrong nine times out of ten? You can save yourself a lot of time and frustration if you avoid doing this. For starters, a foundation of understanding needs to be built up. It's like learning your native language. You learn one letter at a time, then words, and then put the words together. You can then discover themes in words and which ones come to life more than others. You can see when not to use certain words or phrases, and you start to piece your language together. This is exactly what you want to do when you start to define your dream language. Keep in mind this process is done before dreaming. Remember, you only visualize with the lens of context that you carry. If the framework is not in your brain already, it will be much harder to decipher the signified after a dream has occurred.

So, you have my permission to go and study yourself, study the world, study dreams, and study symbols that have worked for others. This will build a big and beautiful catalog of understanding that you can then take and apply to yourself. I will even put some of my favorite definitions and references that I have found in the latter parts of this book.

I love going through some of the oldest dreams that are recorded in time and extracting elements that could be translated into a holistic understanding and application. Much like the dream of Joseph in the Bible we discussed in a previous chapter. The more you practice, the easier your dreams will be to understand. In summation, symbols are to be understood in the context of you and your dreams first, before you try to define them thereafter. Show up to your dream life prepared!

So you're in a dream going through a house and you see a room filled with boxes. What's inside of those boxes? The thing that's inside of those boxes changes every time you see it. It's like the boxes are a conduit of conversation for you to discover new and wonderful things about yourself and about your surroundings. Did it have anything to do with the boxes, really? Or where the boxes are? They're for you to find an element of discovery about a new thing. That is how signified works.

## True or false

Oh, I love talking about dreams! Dreams come alive right before our eyes. They are captivating and amazing in so many ways. In our dreams, we find ourselves making decisions about what is right and what is wrong. We analyze what is true and what is false, in each and every dream.

This is a very normal thing to do, and it is an excellent process to have. However, what you believe to be true is not necessarily what I believe to be true. My truth is true to me, but it may not be what your truth is. See, facts are just facts, until we add our perspective to them. Then it becomes our personal truth, which is a mixture of our mind, will, emotions, and facts.

What is true is not "true." It's what I agree with. What is false is not actually "false." It's what I can't entirely agree with. This understanding helps me realize that I am not God and that other people see the world differently. They may have stronger beliefs about something than I do. They may have a different perspective on life than I do. My dreams are for me and need to be interpreted through my lens of understanding. If I have a firm conviction in my life or dreams, should I hold others to that same conviction? If I discover a symbol to have a very definitive understanding to me, should I persuade others of this fact? My truth is just that, my truth. Your truth is just that, your truth. We cannot remove the relational process out of dreaming!

So you have a dream about driving on the highway. Are your highways wide, or are they small? Different countries have different-sized highways. Some countries have highways that are 18 lanes deep. Some countries have highways that are tiny and they have tiny roads. Did you know some roads in Venice are less than 16 inches wide, and it's considered a road? Perhaps you have an idea that all highways are big. That may be true to you, but it may not be accurate to someone else. We must keep these things in mind when we develop our absolutes. Very few things are absolutely certain. If you said gravity is absolutely certain, I would say the effects of gravity vary based on how high you are in the sky. If you say the sun always rises, and that's certain, I would say you don't see the sunrise if you're in the basement with no windows. You may say there's always oxygen in the air, and I would say it depends on what you have because there are many different kinds of air. I do not want to play semantics, but I want to point out that there's always another story to be told, and we need to have an open mind regarding true and false.

## Were you in someone's dream?

The more people you know, the more authority or exposure you have, and the more likely you will be in others' dreams. 90% of the time, the dream is just for the dreamer. It's not for you (the person in their dreams). The dreamer needs to identify who you represent in their dreams. Why were you in there? Their lens on the world has you in it. They do life with you, and dreams help us work through our life's situations. Lastly, and probably the most common reason is because you are to represent something in their dreams. When they see you in their dream, you unlock a realm of understanding, beliefs, and conversations that they need to access. Who are you to them, and who do they see you to be?

If someone shares a dream with you that they had and you were in it, it has to be relational for it to be beneficial. Don't listen to a dream that has no relational value. 98% of the time, dreams are not helpful if they don't first start with a relationship. I want you to save yourself from the frustration of processing someone's dream if you don't have a gift to interpret it. This book's focus is for you to interpret your own dreams, and they should do the same. Once we get really good at interpreting our dreams, we can then consider the dreams of others.

# CONTEXT AND CATEGORIES

My cousin Tad was in his first year of college when the teacher asked each student what their major was. Most of the students already had a major picked out and a vision for their life. When the teacher asked Tad, he said, "I used to be undecided, but now I'm not so sure." I think this sums it up for a lot of people. Our purpose is in our DNA and is foundational for a successful life. You were created, gifted, skilled, and chosen for good works. You need to know the context of your own life, and then you can rightly apply yourself.

Once you start to see how you fit in certain areas of your life, you can begin to apply the same logic to what you see and how you dream. Context is applied to our life first, then to our dreams. Context brings continuity to our ever-evolving life, perspective, emotions, and situations. Without context, we have no application to who we are and what we are about. The problem and opportunity are that we have individual situations, thoughts, and conversations that would be inherently meaningless, confusing, or misleading if we did not assess them alongside our previous situations, thoughts, and conversations.

Our life is meant to be progressive and continuous. As random as our life events may be, they still have continuity and connection with us. Time holds our life together and ensures that we don't separate from ourselves. If we take one sound bite from a conversation you had five years ago, does that soundbite define who you are? No, not entirely. What if we took that soundbite and placed it in the context of your month's or year's conversations? Would that do a better job of defining you? Yes, much better.

The framework of context provides us with a net of structure and meaning. We can build within the walls of context and understanding. Have you ever seen a clip of news where someone says something and it sounds offensive or alarming, but then you discover the full clip and realize they did not say the offensive thing after all? The clip was taken out of context. It doesn't fully represent the speaker, and it would be hard to have an understanding of their message if only the soundbite was shown.

## The good, bad, and the ugly

Own who you are! The faster you own your entire self, the faster you will apply yourself to life and meaning. Many people encounter various life hurdles, difficulties, and struggles, and they start to partition their emotions, thoughts, and even actions away from each other. This divides us internally and dilutes who we are in our world. The only way to bring the parts of our life back together is through love, acceptance, and compassion. We need to embrace the good parts of ourselves and the parts we don't like. Dreams bring out all parts of ourselves; therefore, we cannot ignore certain areas of our life, or we will never understand our dreams.

We should all get to know ourselves enough to apply work and considerations to specific areas of our lives. With this self-assessment of our emotions, thoughts, actions, mindsets, and desires, we know what we are bringing into our dream life. If we walk into our dreams clueless, then how would we know what we are to be working on, going after, and pursuing? See, we are, in fact, the center of our dream universe. The more we get to know ourselves, the more context and understanding we can apply to our dream life. I believe if you are very acquainted with who you are, who you have been, and who you desire to be, you will be ten steps ahead of someone who is just starting off learning about their dream life.

Being knowledgeable about the big stuff and how you think of it is awesome. How about the tiny things? Maybe you're married. Great! But what do you think about your marriage? What insecurities do you have about your spouse? What do they say that upsets you? What is your collective purpose together? What dreams do you want to build together? What have you been through? If you're married, all of these things will present themselves in our dream lives at some point because dreaming helps us in our life purpose.

Take an inventory of the small things. Don't cherry-pick one element of the dream and forget about the others. Also, keep track of the little foxes, the random thoughts and emotions, and situations that could spoil this whole gig. Are you experiencing outliers in your life, as stated in our dream life in the previous chapter? It's time to keep track of them and evaluate them. They will present themselves in our dream life very soon, I promise you. You cannot hide from your dreams. They always find a way to find the good, bad, and ugly parts of us and remind us constantly. This, my friends, is a good thing!

## The context in our Dreams

Dreams should be evaluated over a continuum of one's life and in the totality of the dream itself. We as individuals should be mindful that our dreams are all connected in some way, even if we are the connection point. Outlier dreams are always a possibility, but not the norm. When we approach the interpretation of our dreams, we should keep in mind the previous dreams that we have had. What themes, understanding, and lessons are carried over? More than likely, we will see a progression of themes and a seasonal approach to the dreams we have.

Each dream we have is a whole unit. It would be silly and ridiculous to cut the dream in half and only evaluate half of the dream. Furthermore, it would be equally nonproductive to only pick and choose parts of the dream that are more desirable to evaluate. The dream is a package; all contents should be evaluated equally, until experience leads us to discard them. If we can keep the unity of our dreams alive, then we will have greater success in understanding them. So make yourself a promise not to pick and choose in your dreams. Keep it together, and you will be much better off that way.

See, you have a dream, and it has many parts to it. It would be inappropriate for you to grab one element of that dream and evaluate it as the whole of the entire dream. That element needs to be held in the tension of the preceding facts and the facts that come after. That is what we call context. We don't want to take sound bites out of our dream and make them sound like something they did not intend to say. We want them to be true to form and deliver the whole message that was originally intended. If there's an element in our dream that we don't like, we need to keep it right where it is so that we fully understand the context of our dreams.

## Thru-line

Individual threads hold our clothes, huge tapestries, and entire floor rugs together. We also have these content threads in our lives and dreams. When a dream starts, the thru-line starts. This thru-line is carried throughout the entire dream, and it holds everything together. It may be hard to see at first, but when you start to pull on it, it will reveal itself just as a thread on your shirt. You can see where it starts and where it is going, with a little interest and curiosity.

Sometimes the thru-line is a person, mood, visual approach, emotion, or present theme. What thru-line is present in your dream? What noticeable element is consistent throughout the entire dream? That is a major key to your dream. If you were to remove this content thread, then the entirety of the dream would fall apart. It's the glue to the entire dream.

Imagine you have a dream where you are being led to go get a job. The person who is leading you is not visible. They take you into one room, then to the next. They take you up an escalator, and to another room, and then to the next. You have one interview after another. In this example, the thru-line is a person leading you that's not visible. If they weren't there, the dream would fall apart. That was the main point of the dream. They were the thru-line.

We are led by this content thread, and it is our guide through the dream. If we are led on a dream sequence, let's stay with the sequence until the end. If our dreams are chronological, let's keep the continuity intact.

## Stay True to Your Interpretation

If your dream starts off as a symbolic dream where everything is signified, you shouldn't switch mid-dream interpretation to make everything 100% literal. That is not how dreams work. Dreams may be mysterious, futuristic, or weird, but they all have continuity. Continuity helps bring clarity. Staying true to our interpretation is vital to keep the dream together. Some may be confused by this because they have literal elements inside their dream that are clearly symbolic. This is why 98% of our dreams are signified. Sometimes the dream points to real, tangible elements like people and real conversations. These elements are literal inside a signified dream. Signified points to things; it doesn't discount real elements in symbolic dreams.

## Eyes of the beholder

Dreams come from certain perspectives, as we discussed in a previous chapter. As we approach our dreams, we should be mindful of the "eyes of the beholder." Who was the visionary in the dream? Whose eyes was the dream shot in? What about your eyes? How did you see the dream first? We want to track through the first-person perspective of the dream holder. Imagine looking over the shoulder of the dreamer. You see what the dreamer sees from the exact same perspective. If you were on the other side of the room looking at the dreamer, you would see something totally different.

This approach should be applied to our dream life if you are the focal point in the dream. What is the perspective that you have? What angle? Is there a reason for your perspective that you should know about and understand? Are you really far away and can't see things clearly, or are you very close? Learning to see things from the eyes of the beholder will help us gain valuable insight. This, too, is why it is very difficult for people to try dream interpretation for their friends because they need to master this skill for themselves, before it can be applied to others.

# Personalized symbols

Our personal understanding of life builds through the seasons and so do our dreams. Every life experience we have provides us with meaningful context that goes with us forever. We may continue to shape our thoughts and emotions around new life experiences, but never forget where we started. The same approach helps us in our dreams. Once we have an understanding of a symbol in our dreams and what it could point towards, it gives us a launching pad to build on. We don't need to start over and guess what it means every time. We can build on it, bank on it, and rely on what it is saying.

The symbolic imagery that we see in our dreams is ours, and it's personalized to us. This personalized context is fantastic and will help us greatly. Keep this in mind as you interpret. No one knows your dream language more than you.

If you have a frame of context around what a cell phone is, then when you see it in your dream, you'll know what it means. What does it do? What does a cell phone mean to you? These frames of context help you interpret your dreams greatly. We have frames of context around many, many things. The more we have, the easier it will be to interpret.

Let's set up a few new personalized symbols. It will be an easy exercise.

1. What are three things you think of when you see a tornado?

2. What are three feelings you produce when you see a candle?

3. What are three memories you have when you see a cloud?

4. What are three pictures you produce in your mind when you think of happiness?

We just practiced establishing your thoughts, feelings, memories, and imagination. We personalize our signified world when we produce a thought, feeling, memory or imagination, and we stick with it. We agree with its form and definition. This means that. This points to that. If we can agree with the summations our lives are producing, then we will stop arguing with ourselves. It's also great to change your mind on what something means. Just agree with the new reference before the next dream. These symbols are our guide in interpreting our dreams. The more we are indecisive, the more we will be confused in our dream interpretation process.

## Categories in dreams

Identifying and categorizing your dream and symbols is a fundamental key to building out your thought life pertaining to your dreams. Every new box of understanding you have, every symbol, every thought, will define your dream life. The more defined your dream life becomes, the better you know yourself and your sense of self. Also, it will make you a really good dream interpreter. So we label our dreams and categorize them for understanding because we care and place value on things. Every dream is not the same. Every symbol is not as important as the next. Through this process of creating a value hierarchy, we find the keys to unlocking our dreams within the mud of confusion.

I have been talking against using a blanket application to symbols through peer think, dream book definitions, and Googling meanings. However, here is my one exception to this rule if we are studying dreams that pertain to our origin and our humanity. Suppose we study dreams of old to find common correlations that we see in our own life. Then, in that case, we can see the patterns and similarities to help us along our journey, and the definition helps us. Please, please, please, be mindful of the slippery slope of blanket interpretation. Your definition needs to come from within.

Suppose we took a symbol like an "apple" and only apply one definition to it. We would miss out on our personal meaning. One person could see the "sin fruit" when they see an apple. Another could see their business because they have a juice stand. Blanket interpretation or universal application definitions should be foundational only in the sense of building us up into our own language. If we're all having the same type of dreams, like "teeth falling out" and "being chased," then there is a reason for that, too, and we should be mindful of the continuity in dreaming. These are some of the top dreams that people have, according to Google.

Through studying dreams over the years, I have developed a few primary categories that would be important to know because they are fundamental to the makeup of our dreams. I have also composed some common and relatable definitions within the categories. I will present to you a few of the more common dreams that you may have, and give you my interpretation of what they mean. I have categorized some dream symbols, people, and things to provide you with a framework for what this language could be for you. Please don't substitute a definition for something that is genuine to you.

## Immersion

As you read through these lists, take in the nuances, angles, and applications. Read to learn how I signify. If you take your time to see it through my eyes, you will gain years of dreaming by soaking it in and gaining another perspective. I truly hope this helps teach your dream language development. This list is by no means exhaustive. It's a list to provoke the signified connection between our common dream lives and dream interpretation. Study it enough to see your dream world signified. These categories are examples for you to learn from.

## People in Dreams

People in our dreams are almost always representatives of things in our life. They signify something we should see in our dreams. If you see someone you know, the dream may be about them on a slight chance; most of the time, it is for you to see relatable elements.

- **Spouse**
  - ○ Intimate, personal issues, family matters, the things you care about most, the closest assessment.

- **Sibling**
  - ○ The context of being relatable or relating to something, similarities, coming from the same people group, blood connection.

- **Best Friend**
  - ○ Relatable, like-minded, fun, what you love to do in life.

- **President**
  - ○ Ruling thought life, authority, ambassador.

- **Pastor**
  - ○ A Spiritual representative, a person whom you relate to God, moral authority.

- **Person you hate**
  - ○ Negative emotions, what you dislike in life, what you dislike about yourself.

- **Most influential figure**
  - ○ What you admire, aspirations, jealousy, who you want to be, something you love about yourself.

## Numbers in Dreams

Sometimes we see numbers in our dreams. These can give us clues as to what is being said to us. Below is a short list of what these numbers would represent in my dream language.

**One** = God or marriage, always present, complete, single, and not subject to multiplicity or division. Strength, leader, first, oneness, unity, beginning, one remains one; it does not change.

**Two** = Multiplication, witness, partnership, friendship, division, family, creativity, abundance, and building.

**Three** = Strength, community, united, faithfulness, group, crowd, revelation, resurrection, balance, pattern, counsel, new life, and unity. Three brings harmony and unity to opposites like one and two.

**Four** = Creation, creative, earth, foundation, grounded, connected, four seasons, authority, government, dominion, calendar, time, and kingdom.

**Five** = Grace or ability, unusually talented, enduring Vision, power, strength, ministry, fruitfulness, fast movement, anointed.

**Six** = Man, weakness, basic skills, average, potential, connection, image, flesh, work, sacrifice, intimacy, knowledge.

**Seven** = Complete, finished, follow through, athlete, ability to continue during difficult times, rest from work, wholeness, order.

**Eight** = New beginning, infinite, mentor, introvert, cycles, stuck in the same pattern, having more than enough.

**Nine** = Gifting, fruitfulness, gatherer, motivational speaker, extrovert, traveler, last and largest single digit. Signifies finality, harvest, concealment, truth, loving-kindness, fruitfulness, multiplication, and the building of the house.

**Ten** = Testing, drifting, teacher, nurturing, writer, stability, divine order, completed cycle, measure, group, blessing, separate teaching.

**Eleven** = Transition, incomplete, wait, prophetic, isolated, strange, in-between number, after the test before the promotion.

**Twelve** = Government, leadership, captain, political, predictable, time, fearless, perfect, order, organization, united, 12 hours in a day, 12 months in a year.

**Thirteen** = Love, kindness, peace, covenant, unity, and eternity. Chaos, and hatred.

**Fourteen** = Development, becoming, growth, naive, reproduce, recreate, disciple, servant, fullness, revelation.

**Twenty-one** = Pattern, responsibility, habit, dreams, wisdom, predictable.

**Thirty** = Full grown, destiny begins, adult, maturity.

**Forty** = Generational, metamorphosis, wisdom, stuck in your ways.

**Fifty** = Forgiveness, fresh start, past is forgotten.

## Colors in dreams

There are three main color pallets that I see in dreams, in addition to the individual colors.

- **Vivid color / technicolor**
  - ∘ Positive dream, divine purpose.

- **Muted color**
  - ∘ Battle for destiny dream.

- **Black and white**
  - ∘ Attack or negative dream.

- **Red**
  - ∘ Love, blood, passion, atonement, redemption, anger, stop.

- **Blue**
  - ∘ Connected, insight, revelation, peace, heaven, depression.

- **Green**
  - ∘ Life, growth, go, joy, happiness, healing, prosperity, money, a new beginning, flourishing, restoration.
- **Brown**
  - ∘ Compassion, earth, wood, humility, end of season, people.

- **Black**
  - ° Night, absence, darkness, depth, Contrast, definition, mourning.

- **White**
  - ° Light, pure, purity, blinded, presence, God, day, glory, youth, angels, completion, triumph.

- **Purple**
  - ° Priesthood, kingship, royalty, mediator, wealth.

- **Gold**
  - ° Value, 50, best years, wealth, riches, tested, refined, sage.

- **Silver**
  - ° Testing, wealth, privilege, purity, 40, generational, inheritance, redemption, truth.

- **Yellow**
  - ° Caution, gift, fear, energy, faith, yield, yield to someone, worry, warning sign.

- **Orange**
  - ° Passion, fire, warning, under construction, frustration, fire of God, creativity.

- **Amber**
  - ° Presence of God, endurance, awareness, power.

## Dream House

You may see other rooms not in the dream house. Think to yourself what is the purpose of this room to me, and build understanding from a signified approach.

- **Kitchen**
    - ○ Fellowship, intimacy, communion, communication, nutrition, relational, growth, development, together, gather, nourishment.

- **Dining Area**
    What are you eating? How quick was the meal? Who are you meeting with?
    - ○ Feasting, business, fellowship, nourishment, planning, connection, unity, family.

- **War Room**
    - ○ War, battle, pain, the enemy making plans, defense mindsets.

- **Copy Room**
    - ○ Remember, (duplicate memories, things, experiences, people) your past, contracts.

- **Dressing Room**
    - ○ Mirror, how I see myself, how others will see me, clothes, identity, shoes, confidence, arrogant, ego, narcissistic, beauty, self-worth, self care.

- **Training Room**
    - ○ Health, fit, work on your image, care for yourself, put in the work, time to push through the pain, get into a routine.

- **Bedroom**
    - ○ Intimacy, privacy, rest, relationship, oneness, marriage, create, life.

- **Living Room**
  The room represents your interpersonal community. Who are you meeting with? Who sits on your sofa? How much space do you have for people? One seat, or ten seats. How many best friends do you see in these seats? What is the color scheme? Muted, vibrant? How big is the TV? TV is the broadcast of commercials in life. Who are you, advertisers?
  - Friendship, family, celebration, entertainment, relationship, unity, laughter, joy, fun, news about you or for you, what you think of yourself.

- **Bathroom**
  - Cleansing, washing, grooming, privacy, preparing, hygiene.

- **Showering / Washing your Hair**
  - Changing the way you think about something, renewing your mind, getting rid of bad thoughts.

- **Laundry Room**
  What are you washing? How much work do you have to do? Did you come in clean?
  - Cleansing, cleaning, washing, removal of dirt, past wardrobe, something new or renewed.

- **Hallway**
  How long have you been in the hallway? Are you alone? What is the closest door?
  - Transitional seasons in between two things, looking for an open door, looking for the next assignment.

- **Windows**
  - Favorable opportunity for doing something that must be seized immediately. It could also mean seeing

what's in front of you; the future.

- **Open Door**
  - Doors that are open no one can shut. These doors are lifetime opportunities with rich relationships. These doors lead you into places where your purpose and destiny are discovered.

- **Closed Door**
  - The door could open up at a later time. Or it could be a way for someone or something to enter your house without you knowing.

- **Stairs**
  - Ascending, descending, promotion, demotion.

- **Swept Under the Rug**
  - He tried to **sweep** his past mistakes **under the rug**.

- **Window of Opportunity**
  - A limited period of time in which one has a favorable opportunity to do, obtain, or accomplish something.

- **Theater Room**
  This is the place of make-believe where we learn to separate our soul from spirit. This is our imagination and our will type of dreams.
  - Putting on a performance, faking it, acting, two face, pretend, creative spirit, host, imagination.

- **Attic**
  - Things that you have forgotten about, happy memories, collectables, family treasures, generational things, lost items, things above your head.

- **Basement**
  What is hiding in the basement?
  - ° The basement is dimly lit, and it's a place where we have stored up hurts and wrongs. We come here to forgive and release those things. Mixed with negative emotions, things we've hidden, foundational issues, past with negative emotions, beneath us, the basement is dark, with no windows, buried secrets.

## Bathroom in Public

- When you're going to the bathroom and the only place you find is in public. This dream is telling you that you need to be vulnerable and transparent because where you're going is to a very public platform.

## Can't Find Bathroom

- When you're looking for a bathroom and can't find one. This dream is telling you that you're ready to deal with some things in your life, and it's becoming your primary focus. The metaphor here is that you need to find a safe and private place you feel comfortable. The great news is that you're about to get rid of some things internally that will bring freedom to your life. This is an internal healing process, and you will notice big changes in your life.

## Cars in Dreams

- You're driving your car, and here are some things that happen. When you get into your car, it's a personal choice. You're going somewhere with your passions, education, and gifts. This is the trajectory of your life's call. It's what gets you up in the morning and drives you during the day. It's your motivation to build or create something that you can be proud of.

- **Turn a corner**
  - To get past the most difficult area or period in something and begin to improve. The end of one chapter, the beginning of a new one.

- **Make a u-turn**
  - A complete change from one opinion or plan of action to an opposite one

- **Miss your exit**
  - To leave in a timely and inconspicuous manner so as not to make a scene or attract attention to oneself. Loss of time.

- **Engine timing is off**
  - The "timing is off" could mean that you are slightly slow in your motions and reactions, or not "in sync" (in synchrony).

- **Run out of gas**
  - To suddenly feel very tired or lose interest in what you are doing.

- **Get a flat tire**
  - Distractions, missing pieces, need to take a break, the environment will run you into the ground, fears coming up.

- **Engine overheats**
  - Anger, thirst, burnout, emotional trauma, emotional

exhaustion.

- **Car breaks down**
  - Stopped in your purpose, plans not working, fear of failure, mission not working. Pay attention to who is in the car with you, and how they are affected.

- **Riding a bus**
  - Like-minded people who are headed in the same direction.

- **Someone else driving**
  - Dreams where someone else is driving your car. This type of metaphor is telling you that you're being mentored by this person or type of person. If it's someone you can't see, you are on autopilot, and your divine purpose is taking you somewhere.

- **Car break-in**
  - If you have a dream and someone's trying to force their way into your car, this is an attack on you personally, who you are, and what you do! This is also a warning dream, preparing you so that you can respond well. This is an attack on you! And it's gonna come after your mind and emotions. This dream is preparing you on how to respond well.

# Office

- Vocation, career, what you do, structure, expectation, order, deliverables, money.

# Garden

- What have you planted in your life, what is hidden in your life, what is growing?

# Planes in Dreams

- Planes take you into a new time and season. You can get on a plane in the morning, and in less than one hour, you can be in a completely different time zone. When you left, it was winter, and when you landed, it was summer, and the language was different. Planes also represent new opportunities, travel, great distance, crossing borders, timelines, and different seasons.

# Oceans in Dreams

- Our connection to nations. Heart dreams, the days to come, issues and troubles that you will have to deal with. The bigger the wave, the bigger the problem. Small waves or no waves represent a time of rest and peace. Dreams of big waves coming towards you. This would bring emotions of being in over your head or fear of failure.

# Outside

- What's happening with culture, environment, politics, economics, church.

# Weather

- These types of dreams are speaking to us about the environment that we're going to be in. Sometimes we go through seasons in life where things are challenging and almost hostile. These types of dreams help us by warning us and alerting us to what is coming. These types of dreams have nothing to do with the weather outside, but it's the storms of life, either at work or in our family. So these prepare us so that we know how to respond to others during these difficult times.

  - **Tornadoes**
    - Destroy and expose through surprise and force, being in harm's way.

  - **Rain**
    - Teaching, heavy teaching, judgment, refreshment, life.

# Different Languages Spoken

- Hearing things that you have never heard before. Your understanding will come in time because you've received the answer, but you need to learn some things before it becomes clear. You are learning to hear difficult things about yourself, so you can change and grow. You're learning how to speak/communicate in a different way.

# Transitions in Dreams

- **Before transitions**
  - These dreams will show you what's coming to prepare you for it.

- **During transitions**
  - ° Once the transition has started, the dreams will let you know how you're doing and responding to the change.

- **After transitions**
  - ° Once the transition is over, this type of dream will let you know how you did during the transition. Oftentimes you will need to go back and fix things after transition, and your dreams will guide you through this process,( e.g., forgiveness and saying goodbye, moving, and getting a new job). Transition dreams are sometimes accompanied by the number 11.

# Warnings in Dreams

- Warning dreams are the kind of dreams that tell you don't do it! Don't move there, don't take the job, don't sign the contract. Sometimes warning dreams seem to be placed inside almost a nightmare-type scenario. These dreams are usually three to six weeks ahead of the test.

# Instruction in Dreams

- These dreams can be very detailed and one to three days ahead of the need. Instructions on big and small decisions

# Purpose in Dreams

- In the beginning, these are very dramatic, life-changing types of dreams. These dreams set the course of your life with strong confidence and direction. These types of dreams will replay over and over throughout your lifetime, reminding you of who you are and what your purpose is. These dreams are a big-picture overview of the plan. They can be three to nine months out from the process. These dreams are tied to our divine purpose.

## Mouth in Dreams

- Speaking, ability to communicate, emotions feeling restricted, intimacy.

- **Teeth Falling Out**
  - ◦ Fear of embarrassment, fear of credibility, and inability to understand what you're going through.

- **Getting Wisdom Teeth Taken Out**
  - ◦ You actually need to get them taken out; wisdom exported, any play on words with wisdom.

- **Disintegrating Teeth**
  - ◦ Losing effectiveness, feeling lost, lack of purpose, getting a new understanding.

## Recurring Dreams

- Stuck in a moment of the past, needing to process your emotions, prompting you to move forward with your goals, telling you to reevaluate decisions. Recurring dreams will stop once you have put things highlighted by the dream, in order.

## Time in Dreams

- Orientation with the dream. It could tie into your current timelines or help you process your dream's chronological journey. Some examples of time are you can be on time, out of time, spend time, waste time, around time, have the best time, or worst time, you can run out of time, and also kill time.

## Environments in Dreams

- Our location tells us things about the dream. We need to think beyond the original purpose of the location and think symbolically. Here is an example
  - An old friend of mine had a dream once about being buried in a parking lot. His employer placed him under the parking lot next to a cemetery. Symbolically, this is exactly what took place in their relationship in the coming weeks. He was kept from growing and stopped by his boss from doing anything. As you can imagine, this was the end of his employment. The boss wanted the employment to be over, so they made it so that he would feel dead to them. The environment in this dream was a parking lot (where people stop) and a cemetery (where dead people rest). Very important symbols to note that set the tone for the dream.

## Keep it in context and use your categories.

Over the years, you'll realize creating context and keeping your categories will be much easier. These areas are defined to help you. You can maintain context within your dreams, and in the interpretation of your dreams you will be far ahead of the rest of the pack. Even the veterans, who have been practicing dream interpretation for years and years, take things out of context. It is vital for you to see the value of keeping things the way they were originally intended to be.

There are many more categories to explore and develop. My heart was for you to see a glimpse at some of the categorical understandings that you can have in your dream language. The list in this chapter was by no means an exhaustive list. That was intentional. It is up to you to define your personalized categories and the contents therein. As you discover your categories and fill in your understanding within the season that you're in, you will see your dreams more clearly. Most of the categorical list I showed you was my personal list. You have the opportunity to make that your own, and I encourage you to do so. But I also encourage you to find out for yourself.

Please keep this in mind as you develop a framework for this. You could get caught in the centuries-old trap of I know it; therefore, I don't have to learn it anymore. And if you fall for that trap, you'll be just like the other ones who search the dream dictionaries instead of learning the purpose of their dreams. I want you to be able to interpret your own dreams in real time. The only way that you can interpret your dreams in real-time is to understand your dream language.

# APPLICATION

Both my grandmother and my mother were dreamers. They would often tell us their dreams and share things about the family and sometimes world events! My mother was a prolific dreamer. She saw many things in her dreams before they happened. This frightened her because she didn't understand the language or why she was shown these things. So she began to ignore them.

My mother and I would talk about dreams, but not very much. I had no idea I would have the same type of gifting where I would see things easily in my dreams. It seems I was destined to have a significant advantage because I would soon meet someone considered the best dream interpreter on the planet at the time. I had a serendipitous encounter with a man named John Paul Jackson in the early 1990's. I didn't know who he was at the time, and I wasn't really interested in knowing him. However, we were introduced to one another through a mutual friend. The day we were introduced, I had five dreams about John Paul. I thought I had the dreams because I was gifted, but later on, I realized I had the dreams because I needed a mentor. These dreams led me closer to John Paul.

John Paul Jackson was regarded as one of the top dream interpreters in the world.. Those five dreams I had opened the door for me to be mentored by him. We soon developed a friendship that would last for decades. I would share my dreams with him, and he would share his dreams with me. He would always say, "That's great. Can you write that down?" He would walk me through the dreams and their interpretations. It's like he knew what the language was for each dream. This is how I started being mentored in the language of dreams.

John Paul would tell me his dreams and interpret them, and I would listen. As I was trying to learn from him, it was like being in school all over again. I was learning a new language. It made very little sense to my western culture mind. It was lots of symbols and numbers and abstract thinking about people, places, and things. To see people not as they are, but who they represent. As he would share his dreams with me, I felt like I was invading his privacy, listening to him tell me his dreams and interpretations over and over. I knew he was being selective in the dreams that he was telling me, but they were teaching me a language, a perspective, and a powerful skill to unlock my own dreams and life.

While getting to know John Paul, I found myself experiencing more of this dream world. The next thing that happened was fascinating. During this time of my life, if I touched people, shook their hands, brushed up against them, or stood very close, I would have dreams about them. I would know and see things about their lives.

One day, I walked into a bookstore and saw people reading books and talking about things. I had never thought about interpreting dreams in a bookstore,but I felt led to meet with the manager, and we began to talk. She seemed very interested in dream interpretation. She began asking me questions about what qualifies me to interpret dreams. I hadn't written any books on the subject, so it was a bit strange to have someone come in and do something like this without a book launch or something tangible to sell in the store. We talked some more and she said, "If you can interpret my dream, I will let you interpret dreams in the bookstore." This was a fantastic opportunity as this was a huge and very well-known chain bookstore, "Tell me your dream," I said. I knew what it meant when she told me about her dream. As dreams go, they confirm what we already know. That's what happened with the manager of the bookstore. I began to speak to her about some personal things in her life and what the dream was telling her. She began to cry. It was pretty intense; she got up and ran off. I thought to myself, "Well, there goes that opportunity." I decided to wait about five or ten minutes anyway. To my surprise, she came back and said, "Can you be here Friday night?" I said, "Sure! What time?" She said, "7 o'clock!" I said, "Okay, great!" She said, "You don't worry about anything, and I will advertise that we will have a dream interpreter here."

That Friday night when we showed up, there was a line out the door. The following day, I received a phone call asking if we could come back the following Friday. They had received so many phone calls about it. They even offered to pay us to come back again. We showed up the next week, the week after, and the week after, for the next few years. So many beautiful things happened. So many people had dreams and destiny's unlocked during those meetings.

I noticed so many people were troubled because they had these dreams and they couldn't forget them. Their purpose dreams or warning dreams haunted them. They couldn't figure them out, leading them to be very frustrated for years of their life. Then, with the current language applied, a simple guide asking the right questions, they could see something that was there the entire time. I went back home and realized what had happened.

I believe I was shown the value of our dreams. How important they are to our life. They are interconnected in our relationship with ourselves, our divine purpose, and one another. Dreams speak to deep things inside our hearts and minds like no other thing on earth. Think about it, dreams are the oldest language known to man.

The story I just told you happened over 25 years ago. Today, I feel even more motivated to tell people about the heartbeat of their dreams, and help them with the proper tools of interpretation. Without it, they will be hopeless and frustrated because they can't get any help with their big dreams.

Throughout the years, dreams have helped me tremendously. I have known things I had no way of knowing because of dreams. Dreams can alter our daily lives if we can learn how to apply them. I dream of things, and I plan and protect my kids, job, marriage, future, friends, and family. We should all have a very high regard for our dreams and our dream language.

After years of serving others, I have circled back around and through this book want to help unlock the dreams of the world with simplicity. I have realized my heart's call, and I dream about you. I dream about who you will become, and how to get you there. Dreams may just be the spark inside us that provokes us to become who we were always intended to be!

Now, let's take some time to review the fundamentals and the foundation building blocks for how we interpret our dreams. We have learned so much in this book, and now it's time to apply it. That is essential for our dream interpretation. Anything that's learned must also be applied. I would stress the importance of this fact because many of you may feel like you already got it and don't need to walk through the steps of practicing. We all need to practice, and we need to apply these principles, over and over again.

Dream, dream, and dream some more. Only through mindful consideration of your dreams can you work out the facts of what they are and what they mean. Only through dreaming and practicing interpreting our dreams can we genuinely unlock what our dreams mean to us. Let's return to one of our favorite places in this book, the Dream House.

Let's return to the Dream House with our symbolic understanding and visit the bathroom. What do you do when you visit the bathroom during your waking hours? Wash your hands, get rid of your body's waste, get naked, shower, bathe, change your clothes, do some self-care and hygiene routines, etc. All good stuff to help us in our day. Now, let's start to signify these elements in our dreams. The same application needs to be tailored specifically to you.

You have a dream where you're washing your hands after you speak to someone. Perhaps the conversation did not go too well, or the dream was dark. What do we know about dreams? We know that 98% of our dreams are signified unto something and probably not literal. Okay, good start. We also know we can learn from the past or others' dreams to give us clues. Awesome! We also know that dreams come from many different places and have different messengers, but they are likely about our current season of life. Elements in the dreams provide us clues for accurate interpretation.

Let's break it down. You wash your hands after a conversation. What are you trying to do? Wash from the conversation. Perhaps uneasy, dirty, nasty things were said, or the topic itself is unsettling. You want to remove yourself from the conversation and make sure none of it is still on you. The washing of the hands is a physical manifestation of an emotional response. You are feeling dirty inside and want to feel clean again. Or you want to remove any guilt or shame attached to the conversation or person. Dark dreams set the mood for focus or temperament. The dark dream tells us how the conversation went without even hearing it.

## Stubbing your toe

You dream about stubbing your toe if you go down a particular street. What do you do with your feet? You walk. Your feet take you places in life. Your feet are tied to your mission and purpose. You dream about stubbing your toe, if you go down a particular street or direction. This could mean you are considering making a decision that would allow you to go down a few different directions in life. It can be a big decision or a life application. In your dream, you get hurt, and your walk gets altered if you choose one path. That could mean your purpose could be hurt, if you go a particular way.

A simple assessment has been applied. Now, where did the dream come from? Then we can say if it's from your divine purpose or if it came from another place, like fear. If you can trace this dream to your divine purpose, then it is beneficial to know that you will not choose that path because you may be derailed if you do. From divine purpose logic, you would feel helped, optimistic, and a sense of direction, from this kind of dream. You would feel guided and known, feeling like someone is helping you along in life.

If this dream came from fear or emotion, you need to sort through it, solve it, and reassess the dream after that. If we apply fear logic to this dream, it would be interpreted like this. See, if I walk and try things, I will get hurt. I'm always getting hurt when I walk. Perhaps, I shouldn't walk anymore. I never liked walking, and now I can confirm it harms my health. I will stay put and not do anything with my life because living is dangerous. The last time I stubbed my toe, it hurt for a year. I may never recover and do anything with my life.

## Dreams give us the faith to believe in the impossible.

Let's do some exercises to help you understand how to look at a dream. In these exercises, we will look at symbols and their possible meaning. In dreams, we all have different symbols and different languages unique to us, our upbringing, and our culture. In dreams, some of these ideas are universal, and that's the way we will do these exercises. It mainly trains you how to think and look at language in a dream.

Breaking down your dreams and reducing them to the simplest form: what is the dream saying? We do this by looking at the focus and sub-focuses of the dream. What is the critical element in the dream that if you took it away, there would be no more dream? That is what we're looking for. Below are some examples of dreams and what they mean.

### DREAM EXERCISE #1

**In this dream, the dreamer visits their grandparents' house and sees all of these things going on. Their grandparents are no longer alive.**

When they enter the house, the front door is open. They see their grandma sweeping something under the rug when they walk into the entryway. They walk into the family room, look out the front window, and see their grandpa mending a fence. When they walk into the bedroom, it's very messy and untidy.

Let's think about what this dream could mean. Remember, we're trying to learn how to look at things symbolically or metaphorically.

**The metaphor of the grandparents' house would represent generational issues in the family.**

**When we enter the house, the front door is open.** The open door in this dream would be an opportunity to change your future by understanding the past.

**We see someone sweeping something under the rug when we walk into the entryway.** Someone is trying to hide their problems from their family or friends, which will not resolve the problem.

**We walk into the family room, look out the front window, and see someone mending a fence.** When you're looking out of a window in a dream, you're seeing something in the future.

**To mend fences is to reconcile with someone** after an argument or disagreement.

**There is another way to look at fences in a dream.** You may have a dream where fences surround your friend's house, and you can't get in. This would be a wordplay that you need to get over the fence or offenses and forgive one another.

**We walk into the bedroom, and it's very messy. .** The personal life or marriage is in need of attention; need to put things in order and take care of issues from the past.

When you start learning dream language, you see the dream as symbolic, but the person as literal. Be aware of these kinds of mistakes, and check through your interpretation. This is learning a new language to stay in the dream language — symbolic, representative. Think of what that person would mean to you personally, as you interpret your dream.

In this dream, the first thing we notice is the dreamer is dreaming about their grandparents, who are no longer alive. The family issues and things of the past are brought to light. These dreams could speak of generational issues that the dreamer needs to conquer. It's also interesting to note that the very things they're doing in the dream could also be things that the dreamer has a problem with. I would say to this person to be careful and work on these areas of weakness.

This dream is seemingly fundamental, but it will help the dreamer in so many different ways if they apply what's being told to them. This dream could save their marriage, business, and friendships from so many things that can easily be avoided.

## DREAM EXERCISE #2

In this dream, I was given change from a faceless man. I knew that what I was being given was from God. I had my hands out, ready to receive, and the change was poured into my hands. I received all change. The amount was $1.80, and it was all dimes.

I woke up and began to understand what the dream meant and how significant this dream was. I knew everything was about to change in my life.

**In this dream, I was given change from a faceless man.**
Most of the time, in our dreams, a faceless person represents God.

**I intuitively knew in the dream that what I was being given was from God.**
I could feel the kindness and the mercy of the person giving me

the change

**I had my hands out, ready to receive, and the change was poured into my hands.**
I was ready to receive what I was being given. I had my hands out; I was prepared as the change was poured into my hands. My posture was indicative of someone who needed help and was ready to receive that help.

**The change I received was all in change.**
In the dream, I could have been given one dollar, three quarters and a nickel, but I was given all change. The change would be internal as well as circumstantial. The change was in change. Everything was gonna change.

**The amount was $1.80, and it was all dimes.**
Everything was about to turn around; the change was 180. When we make a u-turn, we turn 180° around. When we're looking at our dreams, we're looking for hidden messages. So if you looked at the dream and saw $1.80 as the change I was given, you should have noticed this as an essential part of the dream. When you have dreams with numbers, you need to really pay attention to what's being said to you. Next, I received 18 dimes; 18 is maturity. The change would be complete, fully developed, and not lacking, in any way.

The fact that I was given the change in all dimes was amazing! The dimes represented the change was going to be instant because if someone **turns on a dime**, they suddenly change completely or do something completely different from what they were doing before. Another thing to consider is that dimes are silver; silver represents redemption. So you could look at the dream as redemptive, who you are, and what you have been created to do.

Shortly after I had this dream, everything changed in my life.

We moved to a different city into a new house and started a new business, to name a few.

## DREAM EXERCISE #3

In the dream, you're driving your car and approaching the corner to make a right turn. You begin to slow down, turn on your turn signal, and wake up before you get to the corner.

This dream tells you that you are getting ready to enter a new season. When we make a right turn, this symbolizes entering a new season. Usually, if we were to make a left turn, that would symbolize turning around.

Here are some of the signs that you're entering a new season:

You will find yourself lacking vision for the future. This happens because the road you're on is ending. Intuitively, you will feel like you should turn around and go back the other way because it feels like the job you have or your journey is a dead end.

Remember during this time you can't see where you're going. All you can see is a micro vision of what's right in front of you. Seeing every detail can be very distracting, causing anxiety, fear of failure, or feeling a lack of purpose.

But wait, just wait.

This is the place where you meet your purpose. Hold on. This is when the new normal comes! This is where your dreams come true! It's the end of a chapter and the beginning of a new one!

Keep moving forward and get ready. Once you've turned the corner, your vision will come back, and everything around you will begin to change! You are now entering a new season! You will notice a new passion for life and what you're created to do. It will take some time for your vision to adjust to where you're going, but keep looking forward until you get your focus back. Then you will see clearly what's in front of you and what's way down the road. Notice all of the changes around you as you enter the new season, full of hope for what the future will bring.

Don't hesitate to jump back in and review the fundamentals of dream interpretation. For years, we can learn so many facets of dreams about how they speak to us and their true intentions to guide us into our purpose. Some of the core fundamentals that we want to keep in mind every time we review our dreams come from the dream life process. Over the years, I've come up with some fun ways to think about our dreams. Here's a quick reference to what I consider every time I see a dream.

## Dream life process

**Context** of your life. How does this dream fit your life (i.e., education, training, desires, abilities, aptitude)?

**The process** of interpretation is determined relationally! Your symbols and stories are tailor-made for you. Your dreams are in a language that is unique to you.

## Application

The dream is only the beginning of the invitation for you to change, believe, move, and grow into who you are intended to be.

# Remember

Take the time to remember your dreams; write them down so you can return to them later.

# Making room for dreams in your life

Prepare your life to dream. Go to bed at a decent hour so you can have time to dream.

If you are ever stuck on your interpretation, consider the origin of the dream first. Where did it come from? What is the dream telling you to do? Have you responded to your last dream question yet? Do you feel a sense of direction from your dream? Did you receive instructions from your dream? Where does the dream tie into your purpose? Do you feel a sense of caution or warning from your dream?

# Dreams built around the one

Imagine a person standing in the middle of nowhere. And then they put on their glasses. Those glasses are the filter of purpose. They have the perfect lens that helps them see the purpose that is in their life. If they don't put the glasses on then, they never see their purpose. Because they have the glasses on now, they can see what they are called to do. They can notice all the important details they would have missed before. Now, as they look out to discover their purpose, everything within view is the frame of context. If it is not within their view, it is not in the context. If they took one thing outside of their view, then it would no longer be in context. It is like a perfect frame for prized art. The frame must be well intact to hold the art in place.

Now, as this person looks out over the horizon, they can see beautiful things ahead. Some of the things they see might be bright and vivid, or dull, or all different kinds of colors. These colors help set the mood and theme of the dream. The colors they see inside the dream determine the setting of the dream. The emotion that should be understood within the dream comes through these colors.

How is this person orienting themselves in this dream? Are they being told how it happened as though it was past tense, something that had already taken place? Are they being invited into the process now? Is it more present tense? Or are they thinking and dreaming about how it was back then? Is it past tense?

Now behind the person is a beautiful backdrop. Much like you would see on a set of a TV show. The backdrop is the context of time. It always tells us at what point we are receiving this dream. It's like the person lays against the watch. When you look at them, you see the past, the present, and the future. Is the backdrop old? That is from the past. Or is the backdrop new? Then is it from the future? The backdrop of the dream is always time. It helps us to associate the things that are urgent or for now or the things that we are understanding about our past, or the things that are yet to come.

Now we look around and see who the cast is. Who are these people that are playing these characters in my dream? Who do they represent? What are they trying to show me? What can I learn about their presence in my dream that can only come from them? As we start to shape our cast and characters, we visualize the dream's essential elements.

Looking outside for definitions is where we get tripped up. The answers to the dreams that we have are within. You will be continually surprised that within your unconscious, preconscious, and conscious state, you start to unlock the mysteries you have. Within this framework presented in the preceding chapters, you can now lay your dreams on a journey, a timeline of your life. This allows you to look for sequencing that helps you build something beautiful. The outliers are now also more noticeable than ever before. And when you do get an outlier, you know what to do with it because you know where it came from.

Don't overcomplicate the process of dream interpretation. You are now skilled in interpreting your own dreams. But you need to apply the fundamentals of what we have discussed. And have faith in yourself to implement the process. As you trust the process, clarity will come to you, understanding will come to you, and revelation will come to you. And you will be haunted no more by the outliers that show themselves in your dreams.

The process of breaking down your dreams and making them simple is yours. As you get better at breaking down the fundamental elements of your dreams, you will start seeing trends. You will see the common understandings present within your life's seasons. These themes are to be noticed because they help us within those seasons. They help guide us into more profound and more meaningful understandings about our life. Take notice of the dreams that you are having and how they might connect with one another.

Practice, practice, practice, and dream, dream, dream. This is the way to our purpose. Consider it an honorable activity to go to bed and dream. You cannot become the person you are intended to be without first dreaming. So if your spouse is telling you that you are sleeping too much, tell them that you're waiting to receive your next instruction.

Here is a great way to start developing your dream language while learning to interpret them. Remember, you are always going to look at your dreams through the lens of divine purpose. Any dreams that don't align with your divine purpose, put them into a different folder and keep track of them separately. Also, remember that if you are shifting from a sense of purpose to your divine purpose, it will take some time to discern between the two. Be patient. It will take time, but you will get there.

1. Write down the dream and the date.

2. Write down the interpretation.

3. Write down what you think will happen and how it will apply to your life.

Then once the dream is fulfilled

1. Write down what happened and how it was fulfilled.

2. Write down how you were right and where you were wrong.

Here's another way to help you develop your dream language and interpret your dreams.

1. Write down the context of your life at the time of the dream. Did you just move? Get a new job? Get married? Did someone close to you get hurt or sick?...

2. Write down what's going on around you. Was there a big storm or significant event that impacted your city?

I'm amazed at how often I'm helping someone with a dream, and they don't mention major life events at the time of the dream.

For example, they just got fired! Or they found out they were pregnant. We have to look at the context in every area of our life as well as the dream to understand the meaning and interpretation of the dream.

1. Next, look at the dream in light of the dreams that you have had for the last six months. This will help you so much! Now you are looking at the context of your dream life with your other dreams. This should begin to tell you a story through all of your dreams. I will sometimes print out my dreams, line them up, and look for patterns to help me understand what I'm being told or shown.

2. The next thing to remember is to apply the dream to your life. So many people spend so much time looking for the interpretation, and once they get it, they move on to the next dream. When you get the interpretation, ask yourself how this applies to your life. Then come up with a plan to walk out the dream. Just because you have a dream doesn't mean you don't have to participate and work through it for it to benefit you. This is where most people fail. They don't implement the dream. They move on to the next one.

# DESTINATION

For hundreds of years, there were no dreams. No direction was given at night. No warnings and, most importantly, no purpose. This has happened a few times in history. And in one case, it happened for over 400 years. This was to build an important juxtaposition for what was to come. The realization that 10 generations went without hearing or receiving any dreams at the time is profound. But what is even more profound is the generations that came after. Some may say they are the lucky ones. I like to say that they are lucky and they are blessed.

Who knew we would be born in a day that would be filled with so much vision, purpose, and plans? What is it all for? Why would we be born during a time with big dreams? With this inherent ability to hear our purpose and our call? Why would we be positioned in such a way to have this extra form of communication with ourselves and our divine purpose? The answer to that question is truly up to us. But perhaps it is also answered in our ability to have unlimited potential in our lives. Nothing can keep us from growing in our skills, abilities, giftings, desires, passions, or education!

Sure we all have some limitations that we are aware of right now. But, I believe in our ingenuity and know-how we can push through and find the unlimited potential in our lives. Never before have we been positioned in life to have access to so much knowledge at our fingertips. Never before have we had access to the ends of the earth with such ease. Never before have we had such liberty to pursue our dreams than at any other point in history.

This is an extraordinary time. And what you are currently experiencing in life may not be what you could be experiencing if you applied your dreams properly. Your dreams are here to make your life better. They can give you context into the things in your life that you could not see before. That are like a helpful friend who helps you work on little pieces of your heart and your mind. They help guide you down the path of life, keep you from stumbling along the way, and show you the things that could be in your future, so you have something to look forward to. So you have something to put your hopes and desires in.

Dreams are your friend. Suppose you embrace your dream life. Hold it close and care for it. You will realize there is an element of yourself that you have not embraced yet. There is a whole new world about yourself that you are just beginning to explore. You will see and feel that you are unlocked. Your eyes are open. You are informed. You are mindful, and you are an active participant in your own life. Rather than letting life happen to you or situations determine your mood and outcomes, you take the reins in your own life and start to produce the results that you are looking for and that are tied to your divine purpose.

There is an example that I love to live by. It is an old saying with modern application. "You hold the throttle to your life's acceleration." And that is as true today as it ever has been. Ultimately, your life's acceleration is not dependent upon anyone else. You choose how fast you go based on how you apply yourself.

You can take it slow or take what you know and watch you grow.

## Dreams are an invitation into a greater reality for you

The more we lean into our dream life, the more it will deliver for us. As we fix our eyes on the dreamworld, we will begin to see new possibilities in our hearts and minds. These ideas, conclusions, and opportunities can become a reality for us. We need to ensure that we pay attention to the realities we want to create. We can grab hold of our future realities and pull them into our present-day context.

The more ways we perceive ourselves, the greater the context of our understanding about who we are and who we can become. If we only see ourselves in one singular manner, or only in one version, how can we create a better version of ourselves? That is why dreams are so powerful. We see multiple versions of ourselves played out in different storylines throughout our lives. This creates a beautiful context for us to display multiple versions of ourselves at any time in our minds, allowing us to maximize the context of who we are.

## The more you connect with yourself, the better your interpretations will be.

As you get to know yourself better, you will understand your dream's emphasis. If you see some recurring themes regarding past traumas, fears, insecurities, or strong emotions, you are learning things about yourself. Perhaps you should consider getting help to sort through those things because they don't just go away. An unresolved trauma or fear can embed itself into future dreams for the rest of your life as long as it has a hold or place in your life. This will steer your dream life, and it will also steer your future behavior because it's what you are thinking about and what you are focusing on.

As you get to know yourself better, hopefully you are bringing yourself to the place where you are getting the help that you need. Take charge of your mind and don't let your thoughts run astray. Practice having awareness of your thoughts, taking captive those destructive thoughts, and not letting them run wild. And give birth to new thoughts that give life and the freedom to pursue your divine purpose.

Perhaps you have been through some difficult things in your life. I have to. Our destination is not always about where we are going. It is about how we get there. But sometimes life happens to us. Sometimes things are out of our control. And that's true. However, the one thing we can control, the one thing that we do have power over, is how we respond to those things. Our life and our responses are up to us. No one forces us to respond in any particular way. We choose to be mindful of watchmen over the gateways of our minds, our ears, and in our hearts. We get to choose what we bring in and what we let out. These things we have power over. And that helps us guide the ship of our life in a particular way, in a direction that we may find fitting to fill the meaning and purpose that we have in our life.

## Heart's Call

Within our dreams, we will find a heartbeat, a common rhythm that should show us a particular path. This path is for us alone to understand. It is called our heart's call. As we embrace our heart's call, we will find meaning in our lives and in our dream life. Everything will finally begin to make sense. The things we didn't understand about ourselves will begin to make sense. It is not that we are trying to validate every single thought or feeling we have, but that we are trying to balance it against our heart's call. This will help us filter out the good things that benefit us and the bad things that take away from our heart's call.

## What makes you a better dreamer?

Maybe you haven't been the biggest dreamer in the past. That could have been for many reasons. Perhaps you unintentionally shut down your dream life. Maybe you were not in a dreaming season. You may also be a once-in-a-decade dreamer with the most profound dreams. They are all fantastic places to start dreaming again. Today, regardless of your past, you can build a wonderful robust dream life and apply it to better things. My heart's call through the years came from amazing people and many life-changing dreams.

If you want to increase the number of dreams you are having, start writing your dreams down. You will notice an increase in your dreams almost immediately. Also, you will remember the dreams you are having in greater detail. Next, start to apply what the dreams are telling you to do. A year from now, you will be amazed at the personal growth in your life.

Another thing you can do to create a healthier dream life is to notice the color of your dreams. Some of us are more sensitive than others, so you may find that if you watch certain types of movies or listen to things, your dreams are impacted in a negative way. The way to figure this out is to cut things out of your life for a few weeks and see if you notice a difference. If you notice a difference and it is very obvious that it's helping you, then change some of your behaviors to create a better dream life by not watching things right before you go to sleep that could have a negative impact.

To increase the spiritual tone to your dreams, spend time reading the parables of the Bible. This will give you an understanding of metaphors and symbols that will help you dream better and understand more. Reading the life of Joseph and reading the book of Daniel will also help increase your understanding of how this world works. Matthew chapters 1 and 2 will give you some great understanding, as well. There are many different types of dreams in these two chapters. They can help you as you are dreaming to interpret and understand what's being shown to you or what you're being told to do.

Increase your knowledge of your surroundings. Don't be ignorant of the things that are going on around you. Be mindful of where you live, your neighborhood, the people you associate with, and the mindsets in your city.

## Journaling and tracking your Dreams

I'm a huge advocate for journaling and tracking your dreams. The only person that is going to track my dreams is me. It is quite interesting to track your dreams because you realize the chronological journey of some of the fundamental things you have overcome and worked to become. The goal is not to have a notebook full of dreams. The goal is understanding what is being told to you and applying it to your life! But, it is great to have the documented process. I also believe the practice of writing dreams out helps us to remember them because we are visualizing them on paper.

One mental note to consider is that a dream is given to you in your mind. Oh, the bedrock of your imagination is tough to portray on a piece of paper. So feel free to use as much imagery, description, and drawings as possible to give you a framework for the dream. Categorize your dreams in the way they are given to you, and include the elements that are essential because it helps you reconstruct the dream for journaling. There are many different kinds of dream journals. You can even track your dreams on your phone in the notes tab. Wherever you decide to keep your dreams, make sure that it's someplace you will keep safe and have with you for a while. I like to use my phone because it is backed up, and I will never lose them. Also, because it is always with me.

So after you wake up and realize you had a dream, take the time to write it down. You will never remember it as you did when you first had it. There is so much context that comes in the moment. Take the time and write it down. Work through some of the pieces when they are fresh in your mind. Give yourself the space to sort through your dream as you have it. You may be surprised what it will do for your day. Instead of it being an anomaly, it will be a contributor. It may provide you with the solutions that you were seeking. You got to give it to Daylight considerations the implement the dream life aspirations.

## Finding the top ten dreams of your life

After meeting with thousands of people regarding their dreams, I like to take people on a journey of the top 10 dreams of their life. It's a straightforward exercise, but a profound one. The first thing I instruct them to do is to write down the ten dreams that stand out as the most profound. For some people, this may be a simple exercise. But for others, this could be quite challenging. That's okay. Do what you can.

These dreams are profound because they either stick out as completely different, or there is a prevalent element within the dream that makes it profound to us. The dream's profound nature is essential and key to unlocking its origin and direction. If you see any areas of opportunity within those profound dreams, perhaps things you know you are working on or things you experienced in your life, then that would be time for inner healing. If those profound dreams take you into places in the future that you have never considered before, then contemplate those dreams. Embrace those dreams. And pursue those dreams.

A huge factor in receiving new dreams is when we do something with the dreams that we have already had. Simply put, if we realize that a set of instructions within a dream has not been completed, what is the point of getting another dream with a new set of instructions? The first dream hasn't been fulfilled yet. If we detach ourselves from the dream interpretation process, we may be asking for more dreams without doing anything with the previous ones. Once we realize we are at the center of our dream life it makes our past dreams that much more important.

## Establish your start

Dreams are blueprints of our lives. If we see them like blueprints, we will realize their importance and follow them like maps. What is this map of? Is this a map to my heart? Is this a map of my purpose? Is this a map of my fears? These things are significant to help us establish the start of our day.

One of the greatest gifts given to us is the ability to dream. And as we open our hearts and minds to dream more, we will see the dreams flood in. Thank you so much for allowing me to be your guide on this dream journey. It has been an honor to give aspects of my life to you to help you dream more. I truly hope the proposition at the beginning of this book has been fulfilled in your mind. I wanted you to have a simple guide to interpret your dreams. I know you may be surprised about the outcome – realizing this dream book was about you. But I'm glad that you found it and I will sleep better tonight knowing that you will not only be dreaming, but you will be interpreting your own dreams and helping the world become a better place. I am fulfilled knowing that you are out there fulfilling your divine purpose and allowing your dreams to guide you. Anytime you get stuck along the way, take a nap and dream.

For more information and resources
please visit thedreamerguy.com

CPSIA information can be obtained
at www.ICGtesting.com
Printed in the USA
JSHW020345131122
33067JS00005B/18